PRAI

MW00450558

The ... *of the Lord is Unto all Men*

"Focusing solely on the time Joseph Smith lived in the Johnson Home, this book fills an important void in the ministry and revelations of Joseph Smith. Bahr and Aardema help readers comprehend the marvelous revelations, important people, and crucial events in this historic home on a level hitherto unmatched."

—DR. ANTHONY SWEAT,
ASSOCIATE TEACHING PROFESSOR,
BYU CHURCH HISTORY AND DOCTRINE

"I gained a deeper understanding of and appreciation for the Prophet Joseph and many other early converts and critics of the Kirtland/Hiram/Missouri time period. I was impressed with many concisely written details, not treated in other historical works, especially the short biographical vignettes, which increased my contextual understanding of the revelations and events that occurred at the John and Elsa Johnson home and farm. This book is a great addition to the historical, spiritually strengthening treatises of this significant period of the Restoration."

—DR. LARRY L. THURGOOD,
BRIGHAM YOUNG UNIVERSITY—IDAHO,
DEPARTMENT OF RELIGION

What began as a presentation to a local historical society (in front of an audience of less than fifty history buffs), has blossomed into an important new book on the revelatory events occurring at the home of John and Elsa Johnson in Hiram, Ohio. The Johnsons befriended the Prophet Joseph Smith and his family and welcomed them to their beautiful home. What transpired during the Prophet's stay in Hiram led to a flood of new doctrine and modern revelation. That home has been restored, and the events occurring there are now shared by The Church of Jesus Christ of Latter-day Saints with the whole world. Two of the best people we know spent twelve months sharing these events as Church missionaries with a special assignment to act as docents and guides at the Johnson Home in Hiram. That missionary experience, in turn, led Damon Bahr to collaborate with Tom Aaredma, a CES professional and bishop of the Hiram Church congregation, to write this remarkable book about "days never to be forgotten." Carol and I had the great pleasure to serve as fellow missionaries with Damon and Kim Bahr at that Historic Kirtland Visitors' Center (which includes the Johnson Home). Their initial assignment to Hiram led to a request to spend their entire mission in Hiram, which led to their love of all things related to the Johnson farm, which has led to this wonderful new publication. We are thrilled to commend its reading to you and promise that it will inspire every reader. We have looked forward to its publication for nearly five years now. Damon and Tom are not only faithful disciples, but they are also scholars in every sense of the word. Once you've read the book, you'll want to visit the home. We promise!

—BILL AND CAROL WYNDER,
FORMER KIRTLAND HISTORIC SITES DIRECTORS

The Voice of the Lord is Unto all Men

A REMARKABLE YEAR OF REVELATIONS IN THE JOHN AND ALICE JOHNSON HOME

DAMON L. BAHR &
THOMAS P. AARDEMA

CFI
An imprint of Cedar Fort, Inc.
Springville, Utah

ISBN 13: 978-1-4621-4037-4

Published by CFI, an imprint of Cedar Fort, Inc.
2373 W. 700 S., Springville, UT 84663
Distributed by Cedar Fort, Inc., www.cedarfort.com

Library of Congress Control Number: 2021933617

Cover design by Courtney Proby
Cover design © 2021 Cedar Fort, Inc.

Printed in the United States of America

10 9 8 7 6 5 4 3 2 1

Printed on acid-free paper

Contents

Acknowledgments

A great deal of credit for this book belongs to my wife, Kim, who has encouraged and supported me through every step of producing this book. She was an amazing mission companion, and I am grateful beyond words that she is my eternal companion.

I am also grateful for my coauthor, Tommy Aardema, whose love of the gospel and of the Johnson Home shines through these chapters. Truthfully, this book would not have ever made it even remotely close to being published without him. He writes well, is a careful reviewer, and is a stickler for doctrinal and historical accuracy. He shares my love and passion for the Johnson Home and the witness it provides of the restoration of the gospel in this dispensation.

Sharon Black provided hours of copy editing, and Karl Anderson, Seth Bryant, and Scott Esplin, along with other BYU religion faculty, provided helpful feedback.

I also express thanks to Bill and Carol Wynder, who served as the Kirtland Historic Sites Directors, and Michael and Janet Brown, who served as the Ohio Cleveland Mission president and companion while Kim and I served our mission in Kirtland. They provided encouragement and guidance that elevated our service and helped lay a foundation for our love of Hiram, Ohio, and the Johnson Home.

Ron and Anne Romig and Nancy Cervi, members of the Community of Christ who befriended us on our many tours of the Kirtland Temple, expressed enthusiasm for this work, and we are very thankful for the many wonderful friends in the Hiram and Garrettsville area whose friendship and interest in the book has been inspiring.

Finally, both Kim and I are grateful for our family, whose enthusiastic interest in this work has been very motivating.

—Damon Bahr

In addition to those already acknowledged, I want to thank Damon Bahr for his devout example of faith and dedication. It has been a blessing and a pleasure to work with him on this book. His love, passion, and knowledge of church history is priceless.

I would also like to thank my wife, Emilee, for her encouragement, support, and counsel. I gain so much strength from her continued support.

I appreciate my five sons and their patience with me as I constantly share with them the "amazing" stories of church history. They have been blessed to live so close to Kirtland and the Johnson Home. Their lives will forever be impacted by growing up among sacred spaces. Thank you for loving these sites as much as I do!

A special thanks goes to my parents for instilling in me a love of the Savior and a love of church history. I grew up knowing that both were primarily important to them, and it made all the difference in my young life.

—Thomas P. Aardema

Preface

On 12 September 1831, Joseph and Emma Smith, along with their adopted twins, Joseph and Julia, accepted the invitation of John and Alice Johnson to move in with them in their large Vermont-style home in Hiram, Ohio. They moved out exactly one year later, having lived with the Johnsons for ten months of that year (there was a two-month absence due to Joseph's second trip to Jackson County, Missouri). John and Alice (or Elsa) gave Joseph their bedroom, located on the southeast corner of the second floor, to use as an office/meeting /translation room. As it was the place where the windows of heaven were opened in regular and powerful ways, the room is often referred to as the "revelation room."

The time Joseph lived in the Johnson Home was a period of divine guidance and direction. In the ten months he lived there, sixteen complete sections and one-third of another that are recorded in the Doctrine and Covenants were revealed; five additional revelations preserved in the records of the Church were also revealed, and at least one half of the Joseph Smith Translation of the Bible was completed.

President Gordon B. Hinckley referred to the Johnson Home as "a place which will have the mark of immortality in the history of this people," during dedicatory services he conducted on 28 October 2002. "So long as this Church lasts, so long as it goes across the earth, so long as its history is written and known, the John Johnson home will have a prominent place in that history. . . . The power of God that was expressed here and known here . . . has gone over the earth, and we have scarcely seen the beginning of it, my brothers and sisters. It will go forward, and whereas there are 11 million [Church members] now, there will be uncounted millions."

In his dedicatory prayer, President Hinckley continued,

> We dedicate and consecrate the John Johnson home as a place sacred unto Thee and unto us, as a place in which Thou didst reveal Thyself with Thy Beloved Son, as a place in which the Prophet lived and translated the Bible, as well as brought forth under the direction of Thy Son many revelations, and as a place where he suffered so terribly. . . .
>
> May this home continue now as a reminder to our people from far and near who may come to visit us, that Thou dost live; that Thou dost speak; that Thy Son lives and dost speak; and that a Prophet has recorded the things which Thou hast spoken on these premises and held them sacred unto us who live in this favored time.[1]

Both authors of this book have been captivated by the sacred history associated with the Johnson Home. In six separate tours, the first author returned to this sacred place to feel its powerful spirit. Then beginning in June 2015, he and his wife were privileged to spend a year serving in the Johnson Home, joining other senior missionaries in taking over ten thousand people on tours of the home, seeking to enable them to feel the Spirit there. Considering the sacred events that had occurred in the Johnson Home and the dedicatory words of President Hinckley, many of the visitors were visibly moved as they listened to the history and doctrine associated with the tour. The missionaries often heard comments of renewed interest and appreciation: "I didn't know that happened here." "So this is where that happened." "I have known these stories my whole life but now they are real to me." Or, "This place has been the spiritual climax of our Church history tour."

A powerful spirit is present throughout the home but especially in the revelation room. Many visitors were visibly moved as they entered the room; many more were obviously moved as they felt the Spirit

---

1. "President Hinckley Dedicates John Johnson Home," *News of the Church*, Jan. 2002, churchofjesuschrist.org/study/ensign/2002/01/news-of-the-church/president-hinckley-dedicates-john-johnson-home?lang=eng.

accompanying stories of the revelations received there. They returned home to encourage their family members to visit this sacred place.

The second author was, at the time of this writing, bishop of the Hiram Ward that meets in the church building on the Johnson property and was the Region Director for Seminaries and Institutes with his office in the same building. He testifies of the divine influence felt not only in the home but also in the meetinghouse. He has had the unique opportunity to teach and testify in the Johnson Home hundreds of times and recognizes the wonderful blessing it is to be in such a sacred place. He has a deep passion to share this sacred place with others and help them discover the importance of the Johnson Home and better understand the historical significance the Johnson Home has in Church history.

This book recounts the history of the Johnson Home and the people who lived and served God there. It interweaves the divine guidance received there with the historical context of those revelations; the authors hope this account can help readers to feel a small part of the spirit that pervades this sacred place. We begin with two brief pre-stories: the coming of the Saints to "the Ohio" and the backstory of the Johnson family. Following, we address all of the revelations received in the home that appear in the Doctrine and Covenants in order to enable the reader to see the grand story those revelations portray as they are discussed in the circumstances that brought them forth.

These discussions will be interspersed with a discussion of the Joseph Smith Translation, the revelations received by the Prophet that were not published, and one of the most horrific yet faith-promoting events in modern Church history: the brutal tarring and feathering of the Prophet and Sidney Rigdon. The concluding chapter will recount the Lord's hand in restoring the Johnson Home. We pray that you will be blessed as you read of these sacred events and that this work might advance the purposes of God begun in Hiram and throughout the historic land of Kirtland.

CHRONOLOGICAL SUMMARY

1630: Charles II of England dedicates Northeast Ohio to the Connecticut Colony

1796: Several negotiations lead to 1.2 million acres sold to Connecticut Land Company

1798: Moses Cleveland leads initial survey of Connecticut Land Company acreage

1799: Turhand Kirtland given a portion of acreage, becoming Kirtland Township

Early 1800s: Morleys, Whitneys among early Kirtland settlers, agriculture, mills, factories

1826: Sidney Rigdon pastor of Mentor, Ohio Reformed Baptist congregation

Sept. 1830: Parley P. Pratt travels to New York, is converted

Oct. 1830: Parley, Oliver Cowdery, Ziba Peterson, Peter Whitmer, Jr. Lamanite mission

Nov. 1830: First missionaries in Kirtland area convert 127, including Sidney Rigdon

Dec. 1830: Sidney Rigdon, Edward Partridge travel to New York

Dec. 1830: Sidney and Edward Partridge in New York Jan. 1831

Jan. 1831: Revelation "to the Ohio," John Whitmer to Kirtland

Feb. 1831: Joseph and Emma Smith arrive in Kirtland

Mar. 1831: Joseph and Emma move to Morley farm

12 Sept. 1831: Joseph and Emma move to the Johnson farm

Chapter 1

"Go to the Ohio"

The Hand of the Lord in Gathering to Kirtland

T he intent of this, and the following chapter, is to place the
events that characterized the ten months that the Prophet
Joseph Smith and his wife, Emma, lived with the Johnsons
in the larger circumstances in which they occurred. Therefore, the
first chapter deals with the coming of the Saints to Kirtland and surrounding environs.

THE LAND OF KIRTLAND

The "first commandment concerning a gathering in this dispensation" (Doctrine and Covenants 37, section heading) was revealed to
Joseph Smith and Sidney Rigdon in December of 1830, eight months
after the Church was formally organized. At that time the two hundred or more members of the Church located in the Palmyra, Fayette,
and Colesville branches were experiencing intense opposition, but in
Kirtland and the surrounding area Church membership was growing rapidly. Following a general call for the elect to "be gathered in
unto place" (Doctrine and Covenants 29:8) in September, the Lord
said three months later that it was "expedient in me that they should
assemble together at the Ohio" (Doctrine and Covenants 37:3).

Years before Joseph Smith received the revelation in section 37, the Lord had begun orchestrating a chain of events to prepare Northeast Ohio as a gathering place for His Saints. Northeast Ohio is the northern edge of the Allegheny Plateau, which in 1630 was part of four million acres of land dedicated by King Charles II of England to the Connecticut Colony. Following the American Revolution, the state of Connecticut exchanged acreage for federal assumption of its debt, and the remaining 3,366.921 acres became known as the Western Reserve. The Reserve set aside the westernmost 500,000 acres, known as the Firelands, to compensate its citizens whose property had been destroyed by the British during the war. In 1796 the remaining 1.2 million acres were sold to a group of private speculators known as the Connecticut Land Company.[1]

By 1798, expeditions sponsored by the Connecticut Land Company and led by Moses Cleveland began surveying this densely forested frontier. Turhand Kirtland, one of the surveyors, received a portion of the land as payment for his work, and by the fall of 1799 he was selling parcels to settlers in the area that would become known as Kirtland Township. Among these early settlers to Kirtland were Isaac and Lucy Morley and Newell and Elizabeth Ann Whitney, who would later join the Church and contribute significantly to its early history. Kirtland's economy was based primarily on agriculture, but there were also a number of water wheel-powered mills and factories on the east branch of the Chagrin River in an area referred to by the locals as Kirtland Mills.[2]

CONVERSIONS OF SIDNEY RIGDON AND PARLEY P. PRATT

In the early 1800s "an unusual excitement on the subject of religion" (Joseph Smith History 1:5) swept through Northern Ohio, along with western New York and northern Pennsylvania, led by

---

1.   Ohio History Central, *Connecticut Land Company*, ohiohistorycentral.org/w/ Connecticut_Land_Company
2.   "Kirtland Mills," *The Joseph Smith Papers*, josephsmithpapers.org/place/ kirtland-mills-post-office-kirtland-township-ohio

Methodists, Presbyterians, and Baptists. Among those stirring up this "unusual excitement" was Sidney Rigdon,[3] a Baptist convert who had qualified himself to become a licensed preacher with the regular Baptists and began preaching in 1819 in Trunbull County, Ohio. There he married Phebe Brooks, then moved to Pennsylvania in 1821, where he was appointed pastor of the First Baptist Church in Pittsburgh and became well known for his dynamic preaching. A year earlier he had associated himself with the Restorationist movement led by Walter Scott and Alexander Campbell, whose followers were known as Reform Baptists or Campbellites. In 1824 he ceased preaching for the Baptists over the doctrine of infant damnation and worked as a tanner in Pennsylvania until 1826 when he moved his family to Ohio. Sidney began preaching as a Restorationist preacher in Mentor that same year, although he was no longer authorized by the regular Baptists. In 1830, due to differences over having "all things in common" (Acts 4:32) and receiving spiritual gifts, Sidney broke with Campbell and Scott to lead congregations designated as Rigdonites. One of Sidney's proselytes was Parley P. Pratt.

While preaching of a future gospel restoration, Sydney was unaware that the Lord had already begun restoring His Church to the earth in western New York and northern Pennsylvania. Nor was he aware that the Lord was directing him as an instrument to help prepare the way for the fulness of the restored gospel to come to "the Ohio." Through divine orchestration, Sidney's and Parley's friendship would be instrumental in fulfilling that preparatory work.

In the summer of 1830, Parley P. Pratt felt impressed to sell his home in Amherst, Ohio, and travel to New York to preach the gospel. Having only ten dollars, Parley and his wife, Thankful, traveled by boat from Cleveland to Buffalo and on the Erie Canal toward Albany.[4] Along the way, Parley felt prompted to leave the canal boat at Newark, New York, ten miles east of Palmyra, leaving Thankful to travel on to

---

3.   "History of Joseph Smith," *Times and Seasons*, 4(12), 177.
4.   Parley Parker Pratt, *The Autobiography of Parley Parker Pratt, One of the Twelve Apostles of the Church of Jesus Christ of Latter-day Saints: Embracing His Life, Ministry and Travels, With Extracts, in Prose and Verse, From His Miscellaneous Writings,* ed. Parley P. Pratt (Chicago, IL: Law, King & Law, 1888), 31–32.

their final destination alone. "I informed my wife that, notwithstanding our passage being paid through the whole distance, yet I must leave the boat and her to pursue her passage to our friends; while I would stop awhile in the region. Why, I did not know; but so it was plainly manifest by the Spirt to me. I said to her, 'we part for a season; go and visit our friends in our native place; I will come soon, but how soon I know not; for I have a work to do in this region of country, and what it is, or how long it will take to perform it, I know not; but I will come when it is performed.'"[5]

After just a few days, Parley was introduced to the Book of Mormon by a Baptist deacon named Hamblin, which dramatically changed the course of his life. He later wrote, "I read all day; eating was a burden, I had no desire for food; sleep was a burden when the night came, for I preferred reading to sleep. . . . I knew and comprehended that the book was true. . . . My joy was now full."[6]

Parley then traveled to Palmyra, hoping to meet the Prophet, but instead found the Prophet's brother Hyrum, who taught him the gospel. Parley was baptized by Oliver Cowdery on 1 September 1830. Ultimately Parley's conversion led to the conversion of Sidney Rigdon and the subsequent gathering of the New York Saints to Kirtland.

MISSIONARY SUCCESS IN KIRTLAND

During the month of Parley's baptism, a conflict arose regarding revelation and church governance. Hiram Page, who had become a member of the Whitmer family when he married Catherine Whitmer, claimed to be receiving revelation for the Church through a seer stone. Despite the fact that the Lord had directed on the day the Church was organized that the Saints should "give heed unto all [Joseph's] words and commandments which he shall give unto you as he receiveth them" (Doctrine and Covenants 21:4), Hiram influenced many Church members, including Oliver Cowdery.

The Page deception was no small matter for Joseph. As he sought divine help just prior to the September Church conference, the Lord

---

5. Ibid., 36.
6. Ibid., 36–37.

spoke through Joseph to Oliver: "No one shall be appointed to receive commandments and revelations in this church excepting my servant Joseph Smith, Jun." (Doctrine and Covenants 28:2). The Lord then directed Oliver to tell Hiram "that those things which he hath written from that stone are not of me" (verses 11–12, 14). Perhaps expressing faith in Oliver despite his error, the Lord called Oliver on a mission to "go unto the Lamanites" (verse 8) to "the borders by the Lamanites" (verse 9), the area where the western border of the new state of Missouri met the unincorporated Indian territory that later became the state of Kansas. (He also revealed the general location of the city of Zion.)

Three other brethren were called to serve as Oliver's companions in sections 30 and 32. Peter Whitmer Jr., a son of Peter Sr. and Mary Whitmer, the couple whose home was a residence for Joseph while he completed the Book of Mormon translation and the place where the Church was formally organized, was the first to be called. Oliver and Peter were joined by Parley P. Pratt and Ziba Peterson, who was privileged to be called on two missions with Oliver Cowdery but remained active in the Church only two or three years. Bolstered by the promise "I myself will go with them" (Doctrine and Covenants 32:3), and carrying carpet bags full of copies of the Book of Mormon, the four missionary companions left New York in early October and traveled about 1,500 miles, mostly by foot, to Missouri, preaching to various Indian tribes along the way. Their arrival in Missouri was an important event in Church history, but their stop in Ohio on the way became a pivotal moment that would change the course of Church development.

While traveling through northern Ohio, Parley suggested they visit his former religious mentor, Sidney Rigdon. Initially the missionaries had very little success in the Kirtland area, including limited response from Sidney and his congregation, but as reported by Parley, "The people thronged us night and day, insomuch that we had no time for rest and retirement. . . . Thousands flocked about us daily; some to be taught, some for curiosity, some to obey the gospel, and some to dispute or resist it."[7] According to Parley, during the three

---

7. Ibid., 38.

weeks the missionaries were in the area, 127 people were baptized,[8] eventually including Sidney Rigdon and about one hundred members of his Mentor congregation.[9]

Sidney's conversion meant sacrificing a popular, influential, and lucrative position for a second time. Referring to Sidney's position and his conversion, Joseph's history explained: "At present, the honors and applause of the world were showered down upon him, his wants were abundantly supplied, and were anticipated. . . . But if he should unite with the Church of Christ, his prospects of wealth and affluence would vanish; his family dependent upon him for support, must necessarily share his humiliation and poverty."[10]

Sidney and his wife, Phebe, weighed carefully the risk and the reason. "My Dear, you have once followed me into poverty, are you again willing to do the same? She answered, 'I have weighed the matter, I have contemplated the circumstances in which we may be placed, I have counted the cost, and I am perfectly satisfied to follow you. Yea, it is my desire to do the will of God, come life or come death.'"[11]

The missionaries continued their journey west, leaving the new converts to the leadership of four of their fellow converts who had been called to preside over branches in the area: Kirtland, Isaac Morley (later replaced by John Whitmer); Mentor, Sidney Rigdon; Warrensville, John Murdock; and perhaps a fourth branch in Mayfield, unknown in organization or leader.[12] Missionary work also continued as the new converts preached the gospel in northern Ohio, some without formal mission calls. By 2 February, a total of about 400 people had joined the Church, including approximately seventy baptized by John Murdock.[13]

---

8. Ibid., 50.
9. Ibid., 50
10. "History of Joseph Smith," *The Millennial Star*, 5(2), 17.
11. Ibid.
12. "Mayfield Township, Ohio," *The Joseph Smith Papers*, josephsmithpapers.org/place/mayfield-township-ohio
13. "John Murdock, 1792–1871," An Abridged Record of the Life of John Murdock, Taken from His Journal By Himself. Containing an Account of His Genealogy and that of His Children, as also His Travels, Experience, Ordinations, callings, preaching, blessings. Endowments, and etc., accessed 17 December 2019, boap.org/LDS/Early-Saints/JMurdock.html

Desiring to meet Joseph Smith in December of 1830, Sidney Rigdon and an interested investigator and friend, Edward Partridge of nearby Painesville, traveled to New York. After meeting the Prophet, Edward was baptized, and subsequently Joseph received two revelations, one for each new convert. Addressing Sidney, the Lord compared him to John the Baptist and honored the work he had done before his conversion: "Behold thou wast sent forth, even as John, to prepare the way before me, and before Elijah which should come, and thou knewest it not" (Doctrine and Covenants 35:11). Although Sidney was unaware of his role, his congregation-building in Northeast Ohio had prepared the area for the gathering of the Church to Ohio, where the Lord continued to restore the fulness of the gospel. Many of the early Ohio converts had been followers of Sidney Rigdon, who had taught them "restoration doctrine," thus preparing the way for the Lamanite missionaries' success.

In December 1830, Joseph was struggling to deal with the constant and vicious persecution he and the Saints were facing in New York and northern Pennsylvania. After hearing that the gospel was rapidly gaining strength in Ohio, he petitioned the Lord in prayer and received the revelation discussed above that the Saints "should assemble together at the Ohio." On 2 January 1831, the Prophet read this revelation to the members who were participating in a conference of the Church in Fayette, New York, and received two additional revelations wherein the Lord reiterated His command to "go to the Ohio" (Doctrine and Covenants 38:32), promising that "inasmuch as my people shall assemble themselves at the Ohio, I have kept in store a blessing such as is not known among the children of men" (Doctrine and Covenants 39:15).

GATHERING

Many of the New York Saints began preparations to move to Ohio in response to the command to gather. Acting on directions from Joseph to assess the condition of the Saints there and to do what he could to strengthen them, John Whitmer was the first to move, arriving in mid-January. Joseph left for Kirtland by sleigh on 24 January with his wife, Emma, who was pregnant with twins, and a young woman who assisted her, whose name is unknown. They arrived sometime between 1 and 4 February, accompanied by Sidney Rigdon, Edward Partridge, Ezra Thayre, and Joseph Knight Sr., all traveling in a wagon full of copies of the Book of Mormon. As the wagon moved slowly, Sidney Rigdon went on ahead of the group, arriving in Kirtland on 30 January.[14]

When Joseph's group arrived, they parked outside Newell K. Whitney's store, where Joseph entered and greeted Newell: "Newell K. Whitney, thou art the man,"[15] to which Newell replied, "I could not call you by name as you have me." Joseph answered, "I am Joseph the Prophet; you have prayed me here, now what do you want of me?"[16] Joseph had seen in vision Newell on his knees praying for the Prophet to come.

Most of the estimated 200 or more New York and Pennsylvania Saints followed the command and gathered to Ohio, despite, as Newell Knight wrote, that they "were obliged to make great sacrifices of our property."[17] They traveled with members of one of the three local branches: the Palmyra branch led by Martin Harris,[18] the Fayette branch by Thomas B. Marsh[19] and Lucy Mack Smith,[20] and the Colesville branch by Newell Knight.[21] These 200 Saints joined the 400 Ohio converts, and by the time the Missouri migrations began in June 1831, well over 1,000 members were living in Ohio.[22]

---

14. Mark Lyman Staker, *Hearken O Ye People: The Historical Setting of Joseph Smith's Ohio Revelations* (Salt Lake City, UT: Greg Kofford Books, 2009), 96.

15. Orson F. Whitney, "The Aaronic Priesthood (Newell K. Whitney)," *Contributor*, 6(4) (January 1885), 125. Although commonly cited, there is some concern among historians about the authenticity of the phrase "Thou Art the Man;" see Mark Lyman Staker, "Newell K. Whitney: Thou Art the Man," *BYU Studies Quarterly* 42(1) (2003), 131.

16. Elizabeth Ann Whitney, "A Leaf from an Autobiography, Continued," *Woman's Exponent* 7(7) (September 1, 1878), 51.

17. Newel Knight. *Autobiography and Journal*, ca. 1846. CHL. MS 767.

18. "Harris, Martin: Biography," *The Joseph Smith Papers*, josephsmithpapers.org/person/martin-harris

19. "Marsh, Thomas Baldwin: Biography," *The Joseph Smith Papers*, josephsmithpapers.org/person/thomas-baldwin-marsh

20. "Smith, Lucy Mack: Biography," *The Joseph Smith Papers*, josephsmithpapers.org/person/lucy-mack-smith

21. "Knight, Newel: Biography," *The Joseph Smith Papers*, josephsmithpapers.org/person/newel-knight.

22. Pratt, *Autobiography*, 64.

As the population of Saints in Kirtland continued to increase during the first three months following the Prophet's arrival, the Lord revealed that He would "retain a strong hold in the land of Kirtland, for the space of five years" (Doctrine and Covenants 64:21). In that five-year period nearly half of the current Doctrine and Covenants was revealed, and most of the Joseph Smith Translation of the Bible was completed. Most of the priesthood offices and quorums were formalized and filled; missionaries were sent into the eastern United States, Canada, and England, bringing thousands into the kingdom; and a temple was built wherein priesthood keys were restored and the initiatory portion of the endowment was administered. Evidence suggests there may have been as many as sixty-one Church branches in the area surrounding Kirtland by the time the Saints left.[23]

During the Kirtland period, Joseph and Emma lived first in the home of Newell and Elizabeth Whitney, then on the Isaac and Lucy Morley farm, followed by the John and Elsa Johnson farm in Hiram. After a year there they moved back to Kirtland to live in the Whitney Store, and eventually in their own home just north of the temple.[24] Although the Kirtland period was characterized by a revelatory outpouring, the year the Johnsons' home was their "official" residence provided an especially significant contribution to the magnificent events of the restoration that characterized the Kirtland period of the history of The Church of Jesus Christ of Latter-day Saints.

---

23. Karl Ricks Anderson, "The Western Reserve," *Mapping Mormonism*, eds. Brandon S. Plewe, S. Kent Brown, Donald Q. Cannon, & Richard H. Jackson (Provo, UT: BYU Press, 2012), 28–29.
24. A summary of Church events in Kirtland in "bookmark" form is included in the appendix of this book.

CHRONOLOGICAL SUMMARY

1778, 1781:   John and Elsa Johnson born in New Hampshire

about 1799:   John and Elsa marry

Mar. 1818:   Johnson family and others move to Hiram, Ohio, establish a dairy farm

1828:   Larger home constructed for the Johnsons

Feb. 1831:   Lyman Johnson baptized in Kirtland

Mar. 1831:   John and Elsa, Ezra and Dorcas Booth baptized in Kirtland; Elsa's arm miraculously healed

12 Sep. 1831:   Joseph and Emma Smith move in with the Johnson family

Chapter 2

"My Servant John Johnson, Whose Offering I Have Accepted"

A Calling to Service and Sacrifice

A t a conference of high priests in Kirtland on 4 June 1833, the Lord instructed the Prophet Joseph on disposal of the French farm, which had been purchased by the Church (see Doctrine and Covenants 96). At this time John Johnson was called to be a member of the United Firm (Order) that was charged with taking care of this matter. The firm, fundamentally a business management group based on the law of consecration, had been established to provide much needed financial resources to further the work of the Lord and to provide for the poor, including some Church leaders. In the revelation the Lord made John a profound promise, referring to him as "my servant" with the blessing "whose offering I have accepted, and whose prayers I have heard, unto whom I give a promise of eternal life inasmuch as he keepeth my commandments from henceforth" (Doctrine and Covenants 96:6). The events in John's life leading to this revelation attest to why he received such a promise.

GENEROSITY AND HARD WORK

John and Elsa Johnson, prosperous dairy farmers living in Hiram, Ohio, joined the Church in March of 1831 and in September of that year invited the Prophet and his family to live with them. The Prophet's family lived in that home for exactly a year, except for a two-month period (April through June 1832) during which Joseph traveled to Missouri and the rest of his family lived in Kirtland. At the Prophet's request, John and Elsa sold their farm the following year to Jude and Patty Stevens and moved to Kirtland.

SACRIFICE FOR THEIR FAITH

Because the sale was not finalized until May of the next year, the Johnsons were unable to immediately enjoy proceeds from the sale, which amounted to $3,000 and a tract of land owned by the Stevens that was southwest of the future temple location. The resulting hardship included being placed on the list of the poor in Kirtland.[1] When the Johnsons were finally able to access the assets from the sale, most of the funds were turned over to the Church and used to support the Zion's Camp expedition to Missouri, pay part of the mortgage on the Peter French farm where the temple would be built, and pay for printing and other Church obligations. The Johnsons' financial sacrifice came at a critical time, helping to alleviate many of the Church's financial obligations, as well as relieve some of the financial stresses heaped upon the Prophet and other Church leaders. Subsequently the Johnsons were also directed by the Lord to give most of the Stevens' former property to Martin Harris (see Doctrine and Covenants 104:24).

The French farm[2] consisted of 103 acres owned by Peter French, which had been purchased in 1833 by the Church for $5,000. It was located on the west end of the Kirtland Flats, extended on

---

1. Mark Lyman Staker, "Kirtland Township/Trustees Minutes, December 26, 1833," *Hearken O Ye People: The Historical Setting of Joseph Smith's Ohio Revelations* (Salt Lake City: Greg Kofford Books, 2009), 626.
2. French Farm, Kirtland Township, Ohio, *The Joseph Smith Papers*, josephsmith-papers.org/place/french-farm-kirtland-township-ohio

the hill on the south, and was initially held as a stewardship by the United Firm. When the Firm was dissolved in April 1834, the Lord revealed that John Johnson was to be given stewardship for most of it, with the exception of a few lots that were used to build houses, including Joseph's home, and eventually church buildings such as the printing office/schoolhouse and the house of the Lord. John then sold most of the lots in order to increase his family's financial security, and he obtained ownership of an inn located on the property. The Johnsons used part of the inn as a store, and John later converted the space occupied by the store back into an inn, or tavern, that was managed by John Jr. Kirtland residents called the area the French farm as late as 1838.[3]

In just a few years the relatively affluent Johnson family had sacrificed nearly all of their worldly possessions to benefit the Church. The eventual donation of the proceeds from the sale of their home had been preceded by providing a home for the Smiths, Joseph's scribes, a number of missionaries, and other associates of the Prophet. In addition, rather than benefitting from the work of their sons Luke and Lyman, the Johnson parents supported them financially as they served missions. After moving to Kirtland, John worked to sell Church properties, served on the Kirtland high council, and donated more financial resources for building the Kirtland Temple.

Joseph pronounced a blessing upon John on 3 April 1836, which incidentally was the same day Joseph and Oliver Cowdery were visited by the Savior, Moses, Elias, and Elijah in the temple. John was promised: "As thou hast been liberal with thy property as befit the saints thou shalt have an hundred fold in the stead thereof . . . and all that thy heart desires in righteousness before the Lord."[4] Long before John and Elsa Johnson made such financial sacrifices and before this blessing was given, the Lord had been preparing them for their crucial role in the Restoration.

---

3. French Farm, Kirtland Township, Ohio, *The Joseph Smith Papers*, josephsmith-papers.org/place/french-farm-kirtland-township-ohio

4. John Johnson blessings, 1836, MS 2524, Church History Library, dcms.lds.org/delivery/DeliveryManagerServlet?dps_pid=IE12295003

EARLY LIVES

John Johnson was born in 1778 and raised in Chesterfield, New Hampshire, on the Connecticut River. He was a son of Israel and Abigail Higgins Johnson. His English ancestors had settled in Massachusetts and affiliated with the Congregational Church. John's paternal grandfather revoked his affiliation with that church, stating that "the word of God is not preached in truth as it is in Jesus."[5] His wife, Esther, used Paul's words in describing the church as "having a form of godliness, but denying the power thereof " (2 Timothy 3:5). She continued, "As I conceive, by the word of God, neither the doctrine that has been preached, nor yet the church, is built upon a living Christ by a living faith; but I rather look upon it [as] a dead faith upon which it is built."[6]

As a young man John moved across the Connecticut River to nearby Dummerston, Vermont, with several of his brothers, looking for work. There he apprenticed as a cabinetmaker and purchased land.

Alice Jacob, usually known as Elsa, was born in Dighton, Massachusetts, on 17 April 1781, the fourth child of Joseph and Hannah Beal Jacob (occasionally spelled Jacobs). Around the age of ten she moved with her family to Putney, Vermont, adjoining Dummerston, where she eventually met John Johnson. In compliance with local law for civil marriage, John and Elsa gave public notice of their intentions in Febuary 1800.[7] In the latter part of 1800, following the birth of their first child, Alice, they moved to Pomfret, Vermont, where they had purchased eighty-two acres. John built a substantial farm, and Elsa gave birth to five boys and three girls, seven of whom survived to adulthood.

---

5. Andrew H. Ward, *History of the Town of Shrewsbury, Massachusetts, from its Settlement in 1717 to 1829* (Boston, MA: Samuel G. Drake, 1847, 170), archive.org/details/historyoftownofs01ward/page/1704
6. Ward, *History of the Town of Shrewsbury, Massachusetts*, 171.
7. Putney, Windham County, Vermont Town Records, 1796–1833, in Staker, *Harken*, 451.

A VOLCANO AND AN EXODUS

The largest volcanic explosion in the last 10,000 years of recorded history[8] occurred in 1815 when Mt. Tambora on the island of Sumbawa, Indonesia, erupted, discharging over 150 cubic kilometers of ash and gas into the air, carried by prevailing winds around the earth. This massive pollution absorbed and reflected sunlight, lowering the earth's temperature and causing dramatic weather changes all the way from China, across Asia, into Europe, and into northern New England. The year 1816 was referred to as "the year without a summer."[9] Frost occurred every month in that year, several inches of snow fell in June, and ice formed on ponds, resulting in widespread crop failure and severe financial hardships for those whose livelihood depended on agriculture. Thousands of farmers were forced to move west to find new land, including the family of Joseph and Lucy Mack Smith, who moved to western New York in 1816, and the family of John and Elsa Johnson, who moved to Ohio's Western Reserve in 1818. The Johnsons were undoubtedly influenced by New England newspapers that had advertised land in the Western Reserve as inexpensive and quite suitable for agriculture.[10]

The Johnsons, accompanied by three of Elsa's sisters and their families and two other couples, left for Ohio on 23 January. Winter travel was cold, and the children later recalled deep snow, but frozen roads enabled travel by sled or sleigh, with the potential to arrive in time for spring planting. They arrived in Hiram Township in Portage County on 4 March, after a trip of six weeks. Elsa, who was seven months pregnant at the time, gave birth to her tenth child, Mary, in May. She gave birth to four more children while in Hiram, but only two of them survived. So many immigrants from Vermont settled in Hiram that it became known as Vermont Colony.[11]

---

8. Robert Evans, "Blast from the Past," *Smithsonian Magazine*, July 2002, *smithsonianmag.com/history/blast-from-the-past-65102374/*

9. William K. Klingaman and Nicholas P. Klingaman, *The Year Without Summer* (New York: Saint Martin's Press, LLC, 2002).

10. L. D. Stilwell, *Migration from Vermont* (Vermont Historical Society) in Staker, *Harken*.

11. Amos Sutton Hayden, *Early History of the Disciples in the Western Reserve, Ohio*

Within two weeks of their arrival to Hiram, John purchased an existing one hundred-acre farm on "Pioneer Trail," the main thoroughfare joining Nelson, Hiram, and Mantua. Some of the farm was already under cultivation, and it had several buildings, including a log cabin where the Johnsons would live while they continued to improve their farm and eventually build a more suitable home. Additional land had to be cleared, probably utilizing a process known as "girdling." The cleared ground may have been used for sizable crops of timothy and clover as pasturage for a large dairy herd, in addition to potato and corn crops, an apple orchard, and a one-acre vegetable garden. The Johnsons may have further increased their income by selling the ashen remains of the felled trees to asheries that produced potash.

DAIRY FARM, PRODUCTS, AND HOME

The Johnsons had the best dairy facilities and the second largest dairy herd in the Hiram area—ten to twenty cows—and they shipped the cheese and butter they produced down the Cuyahoga River to southern markets, eventually eastward via the Ohio and Erie Canal.[12] The Johnson boys milked the cows twice a day, and Elsa worked with her daughters churning butter and making cheese. To make cheese they cooked milk in large iron kettles, stirring the stiff curd constantly. Then they poured it into cheese presses, tightened the presses, and eventually laid the cheese rounds to cool.

With the Johnsons' hard work and frugality, along with John's business acumen, they became one of the most financially prosperous families in Portage County, if not in the entire state.[13] They were able to enlarge the farm twice—by sixty and then by eight acres—and to purchase a second one-hundred-acre farm that they later sold to John Jr. They used their profits to help extended family members immigrate, then to hire contractors to build a three-story, nearly

(Cincinnati, OH: Chase and Hall, 1875, 246).

12. Michael Rotman, "Ohio and Erie Canal," *Cleveland Historical*, clevelandhistorical.org/items/show/52.

13. *Johnson Home Historic Guide*, Church History Department (Salt Lake City: UT, The Church of Jesus Christ of Latter-day Saints, 2009, 15).

four-thousand-square-foot (attic included) home in 1828.[14] This new home included both a regular and a summer kitchen, two parlors, a large pantry, two bedrooms, and a carriage house—all on the main floor. The upstairs consisted of three bedrooms, one of which was later divided into two, a workroom for spinning and making fabric, and a large attic space above the summer kitchen and the carriage house, later used to accommodate many of the visitors who assisted the Prophet. There was also a cellar with a foundation that provided a place where cheese rounds were turned daily and rubbed down with brine. As the cellar was underground, the temperature could be adjusted for cheese production by opening and closing several windows or by burning a fire in the chimney which began in the cellar and extended up through two additional floors and the attic.

FRIENDS, RELIGION, AND CONVERSION

Two religious denominations prevailed in the area—Baptists and Methodists. Some Baptists, including the Oliver and Rosetta Snow family[15] and other future Latter-day Saints, followed the restorationist teachings of Sidney Rigdon. The Methodists, led by the cultured and eloquent Ezra Booth,[16] counted the Johnsons among their earliest converts in the area in 1826. Their neighbors and good friends immediately to the east, Symonds and Mehitable Ryder,[17] who had arrived in Ohio in 1814, were Rigdonite pillars.[18] Symonds' younger brother, Jason, who owned the farm adjacent to the Johnsons, married Fanny Johnson, and this union strengthened Johnson-Ryder relations.

---

14. There is some question as to when the Johnsons built and moved into their new frame home. Staker (*Harken*, 2009, 281) indicates they were in by 1826. Other sources suggest 1828 (e.g., *Johnson Home Historic Guide*, 2009, 15; Michael R. Caldwell, *The John Johnson Family of Hiram, Ohio: "For He is a Descendant of Joseph,"* (Denver, CO: Outskirts Press, 2016, 19).

15. John J. Hammond, *The Quest for the New Jerusalem: A Mormon Generational Saga* (vol. 3). (Bloomington, IN: XLibris Corporation, 2012), 15.

16. Elliot I. Osgood, *Centennial History of the Hiram Church 1835–1935* (Hiram, OH: Hiram Historical Society, 1935), 5.

17. Hayden, *History of the Disciples in the Western Reserve, Ohio*, 221

18. Francis Marion Green, *Hiram College and Western Reserve Eclectic Institute* (Cleveland, OH: O.S. Hubbell Printing Company, 1901 352).

The Poplar Ridge log schoolhouse on Benjamin Hinckley's farm, located less than a mile east of the Johnsons' home, provided elementary schooling for the Johnson children and others of the neighborhood, although some of the younger Johnson daughters later attended boarding school. A newer frame schoolhouse, built on the same property, known as the South Schoolhouse, replaced the log structure. It also served as a Latter-Day Saint meetinghouse for a time.

In February 1831, on a trip to Kirtland, nineteen-year-old Lyman Johnson met Sidney Rigdon, who taught and soon baptized him. Returning home, Lyman announced to his parents that he had joined the "Mormonites,"[19] causing them some concern. They counseled with their religious leader, Ezra Booth, who obtained a copy of the Book of Mormon and, accompanied by his wife, Dorcas, took it to the Johnsons' home. As Marinda Johnson later described, the Booths and John and Elsa "sat up all night reading it, and were very much exercised over it."[20] By the following morning all four of them had experienced the spirit and power of the Book of Mormon. As Ezra later wrote, "The impressions of my mind were deep and powerful, and my feelings were excited to a degree to which I had been a stranger. Like a ghost, it haunted me by night and by day."[21]

Following this experience, the four traveled to meet the Prophet Joseph Smith in Kirtland, along with Symonds and Mehitable Ryder and a Dr. Wright of nearby Wyndham. During a small gathering of members in the Whitney home parlor, the topic of spiritual gifts was discussed, prompting Elsa to ask the Prophet if the power to heal had been restored. She had been afflicted for two years with "chronic rheumatism in the shoulder,"[22] and her right arm had been virtually useless. He replied that healing had been restored but waited until the next day for the ideal time and place to lay his hands upon Elsa and

---

19. Eber D. Howe, *Mormonism Unvailed* (Painesville, OH: Author, 1834), 216.

20. Edward W. Tullidge, ed., *Women of Mormondom* (New York: Tullidge & Crandall, 1877), 403.

21. Eber D. Howe, *Moronism Unvailed* (176).

22. Luke Johnson, "History of Luke Johnson," *Millennial Star,* 31 December 1864, 834.

pronounce a healing blessing by the authority of the priesthood. Elsa's right arm was instantly restored, as strong and useful as her left.[23]

The healing of Elsa's arm in March of 1831, possibly the first recorded priesthood healing in this dispensation, occurred in the same place where a month earlier the Lord had revealed His will concerning the restoration of this spiritual gift. Recorded in what is now section 42 of the Doctrine and Covenants, this revelation fulfilled the promise the Lord had made in New York "to give unto you my law" (Doctrine and Covenants, 38:32). In verse 44 the Lord directed, "And the elders of the church, two or more, shall be called, and shall pray for and lay their hands upon (the sick) in my name."

The two couples were baptized shortly after the miracle and returned to Hiram. Joseph and Sidney soon followed them and began preaching there. Word of Elsa's healing spread, influencing many to attend crowded preaching sessions in the schoolhouse. As many as twenty converts at a time[24] were baptized in a dammed creek west of the Johnson Home. Those converts eventually included all of the Johnson children except Olmstead, who chose not to associate with the Church. When they met, the Prophet cautioned him that "if he did not obey the Gospel, the spirit he was of would lead him to destruction, and when he went away, he would never return or see his father again."[25] Olmstead traveled to Texas and Mexico and eventually died in Virginia in 1834. Other missionaries followed the Prophet and Sidney, and branches were soon formed in Hiram and nearby Nelson.[26] By the time the Smiths moved to Hiram on 12 September, possibly as many as one hundred had been converted in the area.[27]

---

23. Philo Dibble, "Philo Dibble's Narrative," *Early Scenes in Church History* (Salt Lake City: Juvenile Instructor Office, 1882), 79.
24. *Johnson Home Historic Guide,* 18.
25. *History of the Church,* 1:260.
26. John Whitmer, "History, 1831–circa 1847," *The Joseph Smith Papers,* josephsmith-papers.org/paper-summary/john-whitmer-history-1831circa-1847/1
27. Levi Jackman, *A Short Sketch of Life, 1851.* ca. 1851. Typescript. CHL. M270.1 J123ja 18--?.

A HOME FOR THE SMITHS WITH THE JOHNSONS

On 4 February, just a few days before the revelation of Doctrine and Covenants 42, the Lord instructed the Church to build a home for Joseph and Emma: "And again, it is meet that my servant Joseph Smith, Jun., should have a house built, in which to live and translate" (Doctrine and Covenants 41:7).

Sometime in March, before Elsa's healing, Joseph and Emma had moved to Isaac and Lucy Morley's farm about a mile east of the Whitneys' home in Kirtland. Before the missionary success in Kirtland (see chapter 1) in late October 1830, several of Sidney Rigdon's followers had resided at the Morley farm, attempting to live according to the scriptural injunction to have "all things common" (Acts 4:32) When these missionaries arrived, many of the people who became their first converts were living on this farm, and it later became a place for some of the New York Saints to live as they gathered to Ohio. The law of consecration, revealed in Doctrine and Covenants 42, was first practiced there.

In response to the revelation in section 41, a small wood frame house was built for the Smiths on the Morley farm, where on 30 April Emma gave birth to twins who lived less than a day. To ease their grief, the Smiths adopted twins born to John and Julia Murdock, early Kirtland converts. Julia had not survived the birth of her twins, also on the thirtieth, and John, who already had three other children to provide and care for, allowed the Smiths to become adoptive parents to the twins, named Julia and Joseph.

The Prophet and several brethren, including Isaac Morley, returned from the Land of Zion (Jackson County, Missouri) on 27 August, having traveled there in obedience to the direction in section 52: "Let my servants Joseph Smith, Jun., and Sidney Rigdon take their journey as soon as preparations can be made to leave their homes, and journey to the land of Missouri." In the spirit of consecration, the Morleys were directed on 30 August to sell their farm in order to finance Missouri land purchases. The Lord assigned Isaac's brother-in-law, Titus Billings, to participate in the sale. After saying, "Let my disciples in Kirtland arrange their temporal concerns," in order to move off the farm, He directed Titus to "dispose of the land" and that "all the moneys which can be spared" from the sale "be sent up unto the land of Zion" (Doctrine and Covenants 63:38–40).

This direction to Isaac and Lucy to sell the farm meant that eventually all the Saints living there, including the Prophet's family, would be required to move, so the Johnsons invited the Smith family to live with them.[28] Joseph, Emma, Julia, and little Joseph moved to Hiram on 12 September 1831, the day after section 64 was revealed. At the same time, Sidney and Phebe Rigdon and their family of six children moved into the log cabin across the Pioneer Trail from the Johnson Home. Hiram provided a peaceful location where Joseph and Sidney could focus on the Bible translation.

When the Smiths moved in, only two of the Johnson children, Mary and Justin, still lived at home. Alice, Fanny, and John Jr. had married and established their own households. Olmstead was away pursuing his own occupational "adventures," Luke and Lyman were often away on missions, and Emily and Marinda were at boarding school. Edward and Eli Johnson, John's brothers, had come to Ohio to learn about the Church and were residing with the Johnsons. Although short-lived, both of them joined the Church.

The Johnsons welcomed other Church members as well. Vashti Higley, who soon married Peter Whitmer Jr., stayed with the Rigdons in one of the Johnsons' cabins. Peter's brother David and his wife, Julia, who had married in January before going to Ohio, moved into another cabin. Oliver Cowdery resided with the Johnsons for a short time between trips to Missouri. John Poorman and his wife, as well as another local member couple, lived on the Johnson property. The Lord had directed the Saints to provide assistance to the Prophet's family so the translation could progress unhindered, and the Johnsons assumed much of that responsibility.

---

28. Philo Dibble, "Philo Dibble's Narrative," 79.

CHRONOLOGICAL SUMMARY

Oct. 1829:   Phinney Bible is purchased

June 1830:   Old Testament translation begins in Harmony, Pennsylvania, or Fayette, New York

Sept. 1830:   Old Testament translation continues in Harmony, Pennsylvania, and Fayette, New York

Feb. 1831:   Translation resumes in Newell K. and Elizabeth Ann Whitney's home following the Prophet and Emma's move to Ohio

8 Mar. 1831:   Translation continues on Isaac and Lucy Morley's farm; Old Testament translation postponed; New Testament translation begins

Sept. 1831:   Translation resumes in John & Elsa Johnson's farm following the Prophet's return from his trip to Missouri

10 Jan. 1832:   Prophet told to resume translation following one-month postponement to allow Joseph and Sidney Rigdon to preach against apostates

2 July 1832:   Translation resumes on the Johnson farm following the Prophet's nearly three-month Missouri trip; New Testament completed, Old Testament resumed, second pass through translation for revisions and refinements

Sept. 1832:   Translation continues in the Whitney Store following Joseph and Emma's move from the Johnsons' home

2 July 1833:   Translation completed

Chapter 3

"That Ye May Be Prepared for the Things to Come"

The Joseph Smith Bible Translation

The Prophet Joseph Smith's inspired Bible revisions and refinements, known at various times as the New Translation, the Inspired Version, and the Joseph Smith Translation (JST), began in Harmony, Pennsylvania, or Fayette, New York, in June 1830, and continued in those places and in Ohio for fifteen months prior to his and Emma's move to the Johnsons' home.[1] His move there allowed him to work in relative quiet for a little over eight and a half of the twelve months it was his place of residence, having spent two and a half months in Missouri and one month traveling around the Hiram area seeking to dispel the influence of apostates (see Doctrine and Covenants 71 and 73). It continued for nearly ten more months following his and Emma's move from the Johnsons' to the Whitney Store, where it was completed on July 2, 1833.

---

1. Scott Faulring, Kent P. Jackson, & Robert J. Matthews, eds., *Joseph Smith's New Translation of the Bible: Original Manuscripts.* (Provo, UT: Religious Studies Center, Brigham Young University, 2004), 57–59.

THE ROLE OF THE JOHNSONS' HOME IN THE TRANSLATION

Of all these places, the work of translation in the Johnsons' home was of particular importance because although what is known about the translation timeline is not always specific enough to allow for an exact date, it is reasonably safe to say that of the approximately 3,400 changes made in the process of translation, at least half, if not more, were made in the Johnsons' home. As summarized in Table 1, this fact makes the Johnsons' home the place where more changes were made than in any other.[2] The dates on the first and last rows also include translation work on the Morleys' farm and in the Whitney Store, respectively, because the historical record is not sufficiently clear to allow for a determination of the exact place in the Bible that coincides with a move of the Smiths from one location to another.

Table 1: Translation Chronology at the Johnson Home (also includes Morley Farm and Whitney Store)

Dates	Scriptural References	Scribes
7 April to 26 September 1831	Matthew 9:2—26:1	John Whitmer
26 September to 20 November 1831	Matthew 26:1—Mark 9:1	John Whitmer
20 November 1831 to 16 February 1832	Mark 9:2—John 5:29	Sidney Rigdon
16 February to 24 March 1832	John 5:30—Revelation 11:4	Sidney Rigdon, unidentified scribe (probably Jesse Gause)

2. This claim is derived from a comparison of the timeline featured in Table 1 about the section's revisions made in the Johnsons' home and the timeline displayed by the work referenced in note 1.

Between 20 and 31 July 1832	Revelation 12:1—22:9	Frederick G. Williams
Between 20 and 31 July 1832 and 2 February 1833	Matthew—Revelation (a review of previous work)	Sidney Rigdon and Frederick G. Williams
Between 20 and 3 July 1832 and 2 July, 1833	Genesis 24:4—Nehemiah 10:30	Frederick G. Williams

Other facts that are not necessarily unique to the Johnsons' home characterize the work of translation there. Three of the revelations received there include instructions about the translation: sections 71 and 73, and an unpublished revelation dated 20 March 1832. Two sections, 76 and 77, explicitly allude to the role the Joseph Smith Translation played in leading up to the revelations contained in them, and there are obvious connections between the doctrines revealed or discovered in the translation process prior to their appearance in the Doctrine and Covenants (the age of accountability appearing first in JST, Genesis 17:11 and in section 68). Similarly, as shown in Table 2, the case can be made that Joseph's first exposure to doctrines revealed in the Johnsons' home occurred during the translation—either as a result of a revision or simply as biblical material reviewed in the process of translation.

Doctrine	JST Bible Reference	D&C Section
prayer for the coming of the kingdom of God	Matthew 6:10, 13	65:5[3]
cumbered by distractions of some sort	Luke 10:40	66:10

3. Jan Shipps & John W. Welch, eds., *The Journals of William E. McLellin, 1831–1836* (Provo, UT: BYU Studies; Urbana: University of Illinois Press, 1994, 243).

seeing God with spiritual eyes	Moses 1:11, 31; 6:36[4]	67:10
parental responsibility	Moses 6:58	68:25
stewardship	Luke 12:42; 16:2	69:5; 70:3 (also appears earlier)
laborers worth of hire	Luke 10:7	70:12
receiving blessings brings abundance	Matthew 13:12	71:6
gospel to every creature	Mark 16:15	80:1
mansions	John 14:2	76:111; 81:6
Melchizedek	JST, Genesis 14:25–40	107:71
gentiles receive gospel first in latter days	Matthew 19:30	133:8

On top of these connections the Bible translation work provided a spiritual environment that facilitated the revelatory outpouring that occurred in the Johnsons' home.

SCRIBES AND TRANSLATION CHRONOLOGY

The divine direction to engage in the translation is not recorded, but the divine origin of this responsibility is clearly indicated by revelations involving the translation subsequent to his initial work (see Doctrine and Covenants 42:15, 56–57; 45:60–61). Joseph was

---

4. Moses 1 is considered by many recent scholars as resulting from the Bible translation (see Kent P. Jackson, "Joseph Smith's New Translation of the Bible," in *Joseph Smith, the Prophet and Seer*, ed. Richard Neitzel Holzapfel and Kent P. Jackson [Provo, UT: Religious Studies Center, Brigham Young University]; [Salt Lake City: Deseret Book, 2010], 51–76.)

initially assisted in this work by Oliver Cowdery, followed by John Whitmer and Emma Smith, all of whom had gained valuable experience as Book of Mormon scribes. Sidney Rigdon, Fredrick G. Williams, and probably Jesse Gause[5] followed them as scribes, and Sidney Rigdon's handwriting appears more frequently than any other scribe's on the Joseph Smith Translation manuscripts. As the role these scribes played unfolds in the following chronology, the critical contribution the events in the Johnsons' home made to the translation will be quite apparent.

As Oliver began his responsibilities as scribe for the Book of Mormon, he was told he would "assist in bringing to light . . . those parts of my scriptures which have been hidden because of iniquity" (Doctrine and Covenants 6:27). This revelation, coupled with the learning he acquired while scribing the "plain and precious" passages in the Book of Mormon suggests that when he purchased a Phinney Bible in October 1829 from E. B. Grandin, he may have been doing so with an eye toward the Bible translation. Beginning in June 1830, he served as the first scribe and began the translation record with the heading "A Revelation given to Joseph the Revelator June 1830."[6] At the end of the vision of Moses on the third page, Oliver wrote an additional heading: "A Revelation given to the Elders of the Church of Christ On the First Book of Moses."[7] By the time he departed for his mission to the Lamanites in October 1830 he had written nine pages. John replaced Oliver and wrote slightly less than two pages on 21 October and 30 November, and the following day, Emma wrote two more pages. Sidney next took up the scribal responsibility, having been commanded to "write for him [Joseph]; and the scriptures shall be given, even as they are in mine own bosom, to the salvation of mine own elect" (Doctrine and Covenants 35:20) when he traveled to Palmyra in December 1830 to meet the Prophet.

---

5. Historical Introduction to Answers to Questions, between circa 4 and circa 20 March 1832 [D&C 77], *The Joseph Smith Papers*, josephsmithpapers.org/paper-summary/answers-to-questions-between-circa-4-and-circa-20–march-1832–dc-77/1

6. Historical Introduction to Old Testament Revision 1, *The Joseph Smith Papers*, josephsmithpapers.org/paper-summary/old-testament-revision-1/1#historical-intro

7. Historical Introduction to Old Testament Revision 1, *The Joseph Smith Papers*.

Joseph and the first four scribes recorded the initial Old Testament translation on a sixty-one-page manuscript referred to in the *Joseph Smith Papers* as "Old Testament Revision 1."[8] Recommencing the translation after the divinely directed move from New York to Ohio in January 1831 (see Doctrine Covenants 37:1, 3; 38:32; 39:15), that manuscript was filled by March 1831 while Joseph and Emma lived on the Isaac and Lucy Morley farm. About 7 March Joseph was told to transfer his translating attention to the New Testament (see Doctrine and Covenants 45:60–61). That initial New Testament translation was written by Sidney and recorded on a document labeled as "New Testament Revision 1"[9] on March 8 under the heading "A translation of the New Testament translated by the power of God."[10] Shortly thereafter, John began creating a duplicate copy of the Old Testament manuscript on "Old Testament Revision 2,"[11] responding to the Lord's direction: "Behold, it is expedient in me that my servant John should . . . assist you, my servant Joseph, in transcribing all things which shall be given you" (Doctrine and Covenants 47:1). John finished copying what had been translated so far from the Old Testament (see Moses 1–8, Genesis 1:1– 24:41) on 5 April, 1831.

In early April, John began making a second copy of the New Testament translation completed up to that point (Matthew 1:1– Matthew 26:1) on "New Testament Revision 2."[12] When Joseph returned from his two-month trip to Missouri in August, the rest of his New Testament translation work was recorded on this document.

The New Testament translation continued after Joseph and Emma moved in with the Johnsons in Hiram on 12 September 1831, with John taking up the scribe role again on 26 September and Sidney replacing him on 20 November. It was interrupted for a

---

8. Historical Introduction to Old Testament Revision 2, *The Joseph Smith Papers*, josephsmithpapers.org/paper-summary/old-testament-revision-2/1#historical-intro

9. Historical Introduction to Bible Used for Bible Revisions, *The Joseph Smith Papers*, josephsmithpapers.org/paper-summary/bible-used-for-bible-revision/1

10. Historical Introduction to New Testament Revision 2, *The Joseph Smith Papers*, josephsmithpapers.org/paper-summary/new-testament-revision-2/1

11. Ibid.

12. Ibid.

month when the Lord told Joseph and Sidney to travel around the area of Hiram in an attempt to undo the damage to missionary work caused by Ezra Boothe and other former members (see Doctrine and Covenants 71 and 73). Jesse Gause probably served as scribe from 4 March to 20 March, during which time Revelation 1 and 2 were translated. By the time Joseph left Hiram for Missouri on April 1, 1832, he had translated up to Revelation 11:4 with Sidney as scribe. Upon his return mid-June from Missouri, he recommenced the New Testament translation with Frederick G. Williams as scribe and completed it on 31 July 1832 using a stream-lined recording procedure. Up until Joseph returned from this trip, the Phinney Bible had been marked in places where revisions were made, then entire chapters in which the revisions occurred were rewritten, along with chapters in which there were no revisions. At this time the translation process was stream-lined by continuing to mark the Bible but only writing down the corrected passages. (It is not certain whether the Phinney Bible was used for the entire translation process, but it was consistently used when this revised recording procedure was instigated).[13] At the time of the completion, Joseph then noted that "we have finished the translation of the New Testament" and that "great and glorious things are revealed." Perhaps contemplating the daunting size of the Old Testament when compared with the New Testament, Joseph remarked that he and his scribes were "making rapid strides in the old book and in the strength of God we can do all things according to his will."[14] As he turned his attention to the Old Testament he also commenced a second pass through some of the New Testament translation for review and revision. The translation continued when Joseph and Emma moved to the Whitney Store on September 12, 1832, and was completed early 2 July 1833. In a letter to W. W. Phelps, Joseph wrote, "This day finished the translating of the Scriptures, for which we returned gratitude to our

---

13. Historical Introduction to Bible Used for Bible Revisions, *The Joseph Smith Papers*.
14. Letter to William W. Phelps, 31 July 1832, *The Joseph Smith Papers*, josephsmith-papers.org/paper-summary/letter-to-william-w-phelps-31-july-1832/

heavenly father."[15] Although he did not move in a perfect sequence from Genesis to Revelation, Joseph gave inspired consideration to every book in the 1828 King James version of the Bible.[16]

Following the completion of the initial draft of the translation, the Prophet continued making minor revisions until his death. He had intended to publish the entire "New Translation" but was only able to publish portions in Church periodicals.

THE MANUSCRIPT AFTER THE PROPHET'S DEATH

Having actually carried it within her clothing during the Saints' forced removal from Missouri to Illinois, Emma retained the 477 pages of the "Inspired Translation" manuscripts along with the marked copy of the Phinney Bible following Joseph's death. She refused requests from the Twelve Apostles to pass on the Phinney Bible and the manuscripts to the Church, although in 1845 she allowed John M. Bernhisel to view the marked Bible and make a partial copy of the manuscript, which was later given to President John Taylor. She eventually gave the Bible and the manuscript to the Reorganized Church of Jesus Christ of Latter-Day Saints (now Community of Christ) in 1866.[17] After great effort and expense, including creating a printer's manuscript, this group published the translation in 1867 as *The Holy Scriptures.* It later became known as the *Inspired Version,* a label that was eventually added to the official title.[18]

Over the years following the Saints' migration west, many in The Church of Jesus Christ of Latter-Day Saints were suspicious of the *Inspired Version* despite the fact that two selections were canonized in the Pearl of Great Price. However, Latter-day Saint

---

15. Letter to William W. Phelps, 31 July 1832, *The Joseph Smith Papers,* josephsmith-papers.org/paper-summary/letter-to-william-w-phelps-31–july-1832/1

16. Robert J. Matthews, "The Joseph Smith Translation of the Bible (JST)," *Encyclopedia of Mormonism,* byu.edu/index.php/Joseph_Smith_Translation_of_the_Bible_(JST).

17. Robert J. Matthews, "Joseph Smith's Inspired Translation of the Bible," *Ensign* (December 1972), lds.org/ensign/1972/12/joseph-smiths-inspired-translation-of-the-bible?lang=eng#note2–

18. Robert J. Matthews, "Joseph Smith's Inspired Translation of the Bible."

scholar Robert Matthews and RLDS scholar Richard P. Howard validated the RLDS printing as an accurate representation when Dr. Matthews was granted access to the original manuscripts in 1960. The RLDS Church then allowed other Latter-day Saint scholars to examine manuscripts and gave permission to publish excerpts in the 1979 edition of the Bible. Their work now blesses the lives of millions whose scriptural study is enhanced by the availability of the Joseph Smith Translation, moving toward the full enjoyment of "the fulness of my scriptures" (Doctrine and Covenants 42:15).

CHRONOLOGICAL SUMMARY

12 Sept. 1831:   Joseph and Emma Smith move to the Johnsons' home

25–26 Oct. 1831: Conference in Orange, Ohio.

29–30 Oct. 1831: Revelation to William McLellin, the kingdom (sections 65 and 66)

1–12 Nov. 1831: Several conferences—publishing revelations

1 Dec. 1831:   JST postponed to deal with apostates (section 71)

4 Dec. 1831:   Joseph to Kirtland, Bishop's storehouses, the second bishop (section 72)

10 Jan. 1832:   Bible translation resumes (section 73)

Chapter 4

"The Elders of My Church Should Be Called Together"

A Conference in Orange, Ohio

JOSEPH'S FIRST DAYS WITH THE JOHNSONS

Following his return from Missouri on 27 August 1831, the Prophet discovered that many members of the Church had apostatized,[1] and he would need to direct several localized conferences during September and October to discipline members, train leaders, and conduct other Church business. During this difficult period Joseph and his family left the Morley farm and arrived in Hiram late in the day on 12 September 1831. Joseph reported that for several weeks, "until the forepart of October, [he] did little more than prepare to re-commence the translation of the Bible."[2] That preparation

---

1. John Whitmer, History, 1831–circa 1847, *The Joseph Smith Papers*, josephsmith-papers.org/paper-summary/john-whitmer-history-1831–circa-1847/103

2. History, 1838–1856, Volume A-1 [23 December 1805–30 August 1834], 153, *The Joseph Smith Papers,* josephsmithpapers.org/paper-summary/history-1838–1856–volume-a-1–23–december-1805–30–august-1834/1

apparently involved at least some translation. However, later evidence suggests translation actually began as early as 26 September.[3]

Shortly after the Prophet and Emma Smith moved to Hiram, a marvelous conference was held in nearby Orange, Ohio, that influenced subsequent events that occurred in the Johnson Home. It was one of several that followed the first four conferences held in this dispensation—three in New York and one in Kirtland—all in response to the Lord's direction given around the time the Church was organized that the "several elders composing this church of Christ are to meet in conference once in three months, or from time to time" (Doctrine and Covenants 20:61). Those conferences were often extraordinary revelatory events, although somewhat different in format and purpose than today's conferences.

EARLY CONFERENCES

Three New York Conferences

The first of three conferences of the Church held in Fayette, New York, took place on 9 June 1830 at the Peter Whitmer Sr. home, with twenty-seven members attending.[4] Here Church members voted unanimously to approve the "Articles and Covenants,"[5] a revelation that outlined the governing beliefs, principles, and offices of the Church, now known as section 20 of the Doctrine and Covenants. Church officers were also ordained and received their licenses. Shortly thereafter, Joseph and Emma, accompanied by Oliver Cowdery and John Whitmer, returned to their home in Harmony, Pennsylvania, where the Prophet received the "Visions of Moses," commencing his Bible translation work, and where he first began to compile and prepare the records of his revelations for eventual publication.

---

3. Robert J. Matthews, *A Plainer Translation: Joseph Smith's Translation of the Bible—A History and Commentary* (Provo, Utah: Brigham Young University Press, 1975).

4. "9 June 1830," Minute Book 2, 1, *The Joseph Smith Papers*, josephsmithpapers. org/paper-summary/minute-book-2/3

5. Church Approved "Articles and Covenants," *The Joseph Smith Papers*. josephsmithpapers.org/event/church-approved-articles-and-covenants

The second conference was held Sunday, 26 September 1830, with sixty-five attendees, thirty-five more than the previous conference.[6] Around the time of this conference the Lord gave six revelations that now appear in four sections of the Doctrine and Covenants:

1. Section 28, which affirmed the Prophet's role as leader of the Church, called Oliver Cowdery on a mission to Missouri, and instructed Joseph how to deal with Hiram Page's false revelatory claims.
2. Section 29, which records a highly significant treatise on the gathering of Israel and the plan of salvation.
3. Specific instructions in section 30 regarding the missionary responsibilities of three brothers who would have significant roles in the Restoration: David, Peter, and John Whitmer.
4. A mission call in section 30 to Thomas B. Marsh, who would be the future President of the Quorum of the Twelve Apostles.

By the third conference of the Church on 2 January 1831, the Saints were experiencing intense persecution, particularly those of the Colesville Branch. During the conference, the Lord encouraged the Saints to heed His command originally given three days earlier to leave their homes and "go to the Ohio" (Doctrine and Covenants 37:3, 38:3; see also chapter 1) and instructed the Prophet and Sidney Rigdon to postpone the Bible translation until they had relocated to Ohio. A principal reason for this third conference of the Church was to strengthen the branches and to build the Saints' faith to strengthen them in heeding the command to gather.

First Conference in Ohio

The fourth conference of the Church, the first in Ohio, was held 3–6 June 1831 on the Isaac and Lucy Morley farm near Kirtland in response to the fourth revelation the prophet received in Ohio saying that "it is expedient in me that the elders of my church should be called together, . . . I will pour out my Spirit upon them in the day that they assemble themselves together" (Doctrine and Covenants 44:1–2).

---

6. "26 September 1830," Minute Book 2, 2, *The Joseph Smith Papers*, josephsmith-papers.org/paper-summary/minute-book-2/4

Fulfilling this promise, false spirits were detected and cast out, and the first ordinations to the office of high priest (referred to at the time as the "High Priesthood") were performed. Several brethren were called to preach the gospel en route to and from western Missouri, where the Lord said He would reveal the location of the land of Zion (see Doctrine and Covenants 52). Also, as John Whitmer recorded, "The Spirit of the Lord fell upon Joseph in an unusual manner. And he prophecied that John the Revelator was then among the ten tribes of Israel who had been lead away by Salmanaser King of israel, to prepare them for their return, from their Long dispersion, to again possess the land of their father's."[7] John Whitmer further recorded that Joseph "saw the heavens opened, and the Son of man sitting on the right hand of the Father"[8] and was quoted by Levi Hancock as saying, "I now see God, and Jesus Christ at his right hand, let them kill me, I should not feel death as I am now."[9] This was the first of several such visions of deity Joseph received in Ohio.

MEMORABLE CONFERENCE IN ORANGE

On 25–26 October 1831, one month after he and his family had moved to Hiram, Joseph and several others traveled twenty-six miles northwest of Hiram to the home of Serenus Burnett in Orange, Ohio, to conduct a more general conference, during which a number of noteworthy events occurred. Twelve high priests, seventeen elders, four priests, three teachers, four deacons, and a large congregation attended,[10] including several new converts. The conference enabled these converts to meet the Prophet and other prominent elders; William E. McLellin recorded in his journal that there he "first saw brother Joseph the Seer, also brothers Oliver [Cowdery], John

7. John Whitmer, History, 1831–circa 1847, chapter 7, *The Joseph Smith Papers*, josephsmithpapers.org/paper-summary/john-whitmer-history-1831–circa-1847/31#X2B0C8866–2F07–47EC-8C5A-9EF80A6C7C11

8. John Whitmer, History, 1831–circa 1847, chapter 7.

9. Levi Ward Hancock, *The Life of Levi Hancock*, MS 8174, CHL, dcms.lds.org/delivery/DeliveryManagerServlet?dps_pid=IE2354662

10. Minutes, 25–26 Oct. 1831, p. 10, *The Joseph Smith Papers*, josephsmithpapers.org/paper-summary/minutes-25–26–october-1831/1

[Whitmer] [and] Sidney [Rigdon] and a great many other Elders."[11] He also recorded, "This conference was attended by me with much spiritual edification [and] comfort to my heart."[12] Joel Johnson likewise recorded first meeting the Prophet there.[13]

Consecration

Apparently without an invitation to do so, many attendees spontaneously stated their willingness to consecrate all that they had to the Church. They were possibly responding to two of the Lord's commands, the first in the law revealed in the Whitneys' home that "thou wilt remember the poor, and consecrate of thy properties for their support" (Doctrine and Covenants 42:30). The second of these commands was in response to the Prophet's question about procuring land for the Saints arriving from the east (see Doctrine and Covenants 48:2). According to John Whitmer, Emer Harris, the brother of Martin Harris, was first, saying "he was determined to be for God & none else & with his assistance to do his will."[14] He was followed by Orson Hyde, who "covenanted to give all to the Lord and be for his glory and as to all his works his heart."[15] Joseph Smith, Sr. added "that he had nothing to consecrate to the Lord of the things of the Earth, yet he felt to consecrate himself too and [his] family."[16] Several others declared similar commitments.

Ordination to the High Priesthood

The Prophet declared that it was the "privilege of every Elder present to be ordained to the High Priesthood."[17] Fifteen ordinations to the office of high priest were then performed, adding to those who had

---

11. William Earl McLellin, *The Journals of William E. McLellin*, 1831–1836, eds. Jan Shipps and John W. Welch (Chicago: University of Illinois Press, 1994), 234.

12. Ibid., 45.

13. Joel Hills Johnson (ca. 1882), *Autobiography*, MS 15025, CHL.

14. Minute Book 2, 11. *The Joseph Smith Papers*, josephsmithpapers.org/paper-summary/minute-book-2/13.

15. Ibid., 11.

16. Ibid., 13,

17. Ibid, 11.

first been ordained in June. The usage of the term "High Priesthood" in 1831 differed from later usages. In the June and October 1831 conferences this term referred specifically to the office of high priest, and this usage continued until the circa April 1835 "Instruction on Priesthood," now known as Doctrine and Covenants 107.

The meaning of the term "seal" has also evolved. In Orange, the Prophet connected the authority of the "High Priesthood" to the power to "seal up the Saints unto eternal life." A week after the conference in Orange, at another conference held on 1 November in the Johnsons' home, the Lord similarly affirmed to four high priests: "And of as many as the Father shall bear record, to you shall be given power to seal them up unto eternal life" (Doctrine and Covenants 68:12). These statements suggest a broader usage of the term "seal" than the more common usage today.

Support for Bible Translation and Missionary Families

Joseph followed the sealing/high priest instruction with a call for the Saints to repent by declaring, "God (has) often sealed up the heavens because of covetousness in the Church."[18] He then emphasized two responsibilities related to avoiding covetousness. The first concerned the period of the Bible revision. As recorded in the minutes of the conference, "[T]he greatest blessings which God had to bestow should be given to those who contributed to the support of his family while translating the fullness of the scriptures. . . . and except the church receive the fullness of the scriptures that they would yet fall."[19] Joseph and Sidney had to devote their full time to the Bible translation, and others were called to sacrifice to a lesser degree. The Prophet's family was provided for while they resided in Hiram, but a large portion of their support came directly from the Johnson family.

The second responsibility involved providing for the families of missionaries. "The Lord [holds] the Church bound to provide for the families of the absent Elders."[20] Four months later at a conference in

---

18. Minute Book 2, 13.
19. Ibid.
20. Luke Johnson, "History of Luke Johnson," *Millennial Star*, 31 December 1864, 835.

Amherst, Ohio, the Lord emphasized this responsibility, saying "that it is the duty of the church to assist in supporting the families of those [serving], and also . . . the families of those who are called . . . [to] be sent unto the world to proclaim the gospel unto the world" (Doctrine and Covenants 75:24).

The Book of Mormon

Although not entirely corroborated by other sources, Luke Johnson's history states that the eleven witnesses to the Book of Mormon were present at the conference, and "with uplifted hands, bore their solemn testimony to the truth of that book; as did also the Prophet Joseph."[21] (Christian and Jacob Whitmer and Hiram Page may not have been present, as their names do not appear in the minutes.) One of the eight witnesses to the Book of Mormon, Hyrum Smith, requested that his brother Joseph share some insights into its translation process; however, Joseph responded that "it was not intended to tell the world all the particulars of the coming forth of that book and that it was not expedient for him to relate those things."[22]

---

21. Minute Book 2, 13.
22. Translate, *Glossary, The Joseph Smith Papers*, josephsmithpapers.org/topic/translate.

CHRONOLOGICAL SUMMARY

25–26 October 1831:   Major conference held in Orange, Ohio.

29–30 October 1831:   Revelation for William McLellin, the kingdom (sections 65 and 66)

1–12 November 1831:   Several conferences—publishing revelations

1 December 183171:   JST postponed, dealing with apostates

10 January 1832:   Joseph and Sidney to recommence Bible translation

25 January 1832:   Sustaining as High Priest President, mission calls (section 75)

16 February 1832:   The Vision (section 76)

7 March 1832:   Eden Smith, Stephen Burnett mission calls (section 80)

12 March 1832:   Jared Carter mission call (section 79)

29 August 1832:   John Murdock (section 99)

Chapter 5

"Seek Not to Be Encumbered"

William E. McLellin,
Keys of the Kingdom, Mission Calls

DOCTRINE AND COVENANTS 66 AND 65

This chapter includes discussions of Doctrine and Covenants 66, which was directed to William E. McLellin shortly after his conversion and arrival in Hiram and section 65, which very briefly but powerfully details important doctrine regarding the keys of the kingdom. Although displayed in the Doctrine and Covenants according to section number, section 66 was revealed before section 65. It also contains a discussion of the mission calls of Eden Smith, Stephen Burnett, Jared Carter, and John Murdock in Doctrine and Covenants 75, 79–80, and 99.

WILLIAM E. MCLELLIN

On 29 October 1831 the Prophet received a revelation in response to William E. McLellin's secret prayerful request for answers to specific questions, which he used as a test of the validity of Joseph's claim to be a prophet. William served as recorder of the revelation when it was given.[1]

---

1. Revelation, 29 October 1831 [D&C 66], *The Joseph Smith Papers*, josephsmithpapers. org/paper-summary/revelation-29–october-1831–dc-66/1#historical-intro.

The thirteen verses of this revelation include several aspects of doctrine that become more meaningful by considering the context in which it was given, particularly William's inconsistent commitment to the Church.

Background and Conversion

William was born to Charles and Sarah McLellin in Smith County, Tennessee, on 18 January 1806, less than a month after the Prophet was born in Vermont.[2] During his early adult years he was employed as a school teacher. He married Cynthia Ann (no maiden name available) in July 1829, but after two years, he lamented, "I was deprived of her most lovely endeavors to render me happy and agreeable. In consequence of which, I spent many lonesome and sorrowful hours."[3]

William first heard the gospel in Paris, Illinois, where David Whitmer and Harvey Whitlock were conducting an outdoor meeting en route to Jackson County, Missouri (see Doctrine and Covenants 52:25). Desiring to meet the Prophet, William traveled to Jackson County, where Joseph had also been directed by revelation (see Doctrine and Covenants 52). By the time William arrived, however, the Prophet had already returned to Kirtland. Though disappointed, he listened to Hyrum Smith in a private, four-hour discussion on 19 August; on the following day he recorded in his journal: "I rose early and betook myself in earnest prayer to God to direct me into truth, and from all the light that I could gain by examinations, searches, and researches, I was bound as an honest man to acknowledge the truths and validity of the Book of Mormon and also that I had found the people of the Lord—the living Church of Christ. Consequently, as soon as we took breakfast I told Elder Smith that I wanted him to baptize me . . . and [was] baptized the next day."[4] Hyrum ordained William an elder four days later and then served a mission with him.

---

2. McLellin, William Earl, *The Joseph Smith Papers*, josephsmithpapers.org/person/william-earl-mclellin

3. William McLellin to Relatives, 4 Aug 1832, typescript, RLDS Archives as cited in Book of Abraham Project, boap.org/LDS/Early-Saints/Mcllelin.html.

4. Jan Shipps & John W. Welch, eds., *The Journals of William E. McLellin, 1831–1836* (Provo, UT: BYU Studies; Urbana: University of Illinois Press, 1994), 49.

In late October William traveled to Orange, Ohio, to attend a conference at which he "first saw brother Joseph the Seer" and was ordained a high priest by Oliver Cowdery. He added that "this conference was attended by me with much spiritual edification & comfort to my heart."[5] Following the conference, William received another manifestation of the Prophet's divine calling while journeying to Kirtland. "[I] stepped off of a large log and strained my ankle very badly. . . . He laid his hands on [the ankle] . . . and it was healed although It was swelled much and had pained me severely."[6]

Doctrine and Covenants 66

Despite these experiences, William showed an inclination toward sign-seeking when he chose to test the authenticity of Joseph's calling. He wrote that he "went before the Lord in secret, and on my knees asked him to reveal the answer to five questions through his Prophet."[7] Then on 29 October, without informing Joseph of his secret prayer and five questions, William asked Joseph to seek for divine guidance on his behalf. In response to this request, Joseph received a revelation, now known as Doctrine and Covenants 66. The Lord's response included answers to William's five questions, although the historical record does not specify their substance. In 1848, after being out of the Church for ten years, William still regarded this revelation as a witness of the Prophet's divine calling. "I now testify in the fear of God that every question which I had thus lodged in the ears of the Lord of Sabbaoth, were answered to my full and entire satisfaction. I desired it for a testimony of Joseph's inspiration. And I to this day consider it to me an evidence a witness which I cannot refute."[8]

Among the answers to the five questions, the Lord expressed concern for William's iniquities in verses 1, 3, and 10, specifically mentioning in verse 10, "Commit not adultery—a temptation with which thou has been troubled." William later appears to have violated this

---

5. Ibid., 33.
6. Ibid., 44–45.
7. Ibid., 45.
8. William E. McLellin, *The Ensign of Liberty of the Church of Christ* 1(4) (January 1848), 61.

command. He received Church discipline twice for breaking the law of chastity, the second time resulting in his decision to remain permanently separated from the Church.

Missionary Labors and Losing Church Membership

In this section, the Lord called William to "proclaim my gospel . . . in those regions round about where it has not been proclaimed . . . and unto the eastern lands. . . . [with] my servant Samuel H. Smith (Joseph's younger brother)" (verses 5, 7–8). Speaking of Samuel's response to this call, Lucy Mack Smith recorded, "Samuel heard a voice in the night which called to him, saying, 'Samuel, arise immediately and go forth on the mission which thou wast commanded to take to Hiram.' He arose and took what clothing he had in readiness and set out without eating."[9] Samuel and William were "tolerably well received" as they labored together.

Section 66 specifically directs William and Samuel to "lay your hands upon the sick," promising "they shall recover" (verse 8). Lucy recorded the fulfillment of this promise: "They were sent for by a woman who had been sick many months and had prayed much that the Lord would send some of the Mormons into that country that she might have hands laid on her for the recovery of her health. Samuel went immediately to her and administered to her by the laying on of hands in the name of the Lord and she was healed and was also baptized."[10]

In a 25 January 1832 reveleation, the Lord chastened William "for the murmurings of his heart" (Doctrine and Covenants 75:6; note this section was revealed in Amherst, Ohio, during the year the Johnsons' home was Joseph and Emma's residence) after abandoning a mission to "the eastern countries" (verse 6). He then said, "I revoke the commission which I gave unto him . . . give unto him a new commission . . . Go ye into the south countries" (verses 6–8) with Luke Johnson. William abandoned this mission as well, in order to marry Emeline Miller, who, ironically, was Luke's cousin.

William traveled to Jackson County a week following his marriage, where he was temporarily excommunicated in December for

---

9. Lavina Fielding Anderson, *Lucy's Book: A Critical Edition of Lucy Mack Smith's Family Memoir* (Salt Lake City: Signature Books, 2001, 556).

10. Ibid., 556.

relations with "a certain harlot"[11] and was apparently reinstated a month later (January–June 1833) when he began a third mission to Missouri and Illinois with Parley P. Pratt. During the winter of 1833–34 he and Emmeline were driven out of Jackson County with the other Saints who were living there. They fled to Clay County but returned to Kirtland later in 1834, where William was ordained a member of the Quorum of the Twelve Apostles in February 1835. He was one of three members of the original Twelve who had not marched with Zion's Camp.

William was disfellowshipped later that year for writing a letter that "cast . . . censure upon the [first] presidency."[12] His subsequent reinstatement in September 1835 was short-lived, as he withdrew from the Church after four months. After being re-sustained as an Apostle in August of 1836, he moved back to Missouri with the Saints as they were driven out of Kirtland. He joined in the rampant criticism of the Prophet in 1837 and 1838, and his failure to sustain Church leadership left him susceptible to "adultery—a temptation with which thou hast been troubled" (Doctrine and Covenants 66:10). At his May 1838 excommunication hearing, "he said he had no confidence in the Presidency of the Church; consequently, he had quit praying and keeping the commandments of the Lord, and indulged himself in his sinful lusts. It was from what he had heard that he believed the presidency had got out of the way, and not from anything that he had seen himself."[13] He then actively participated with the mobs who drove the Saints out of Missouri.

During the next several years William lived in five different states, then returned to Jackson County. During this time, he associated with various splinter groups that were led by George

---

11. William E. McLellin, letter to the Smith's eldest son, Joseph III, Community of Christ Archives; (July, 1872), copy CHL, M270.1 M1648m 2007; Stan Larson and Samuel J. Passey, eds., *The William E. McLellin Papers*, 1854–1880 (Salt Lake City, UT: Signature Books, 2007, 488–89); Robert D. Hutchins, "Joseph Smith III: Moderate Mormon," (master's thesis, Brigham Young University, 1977), 79–81.

12. "History and Writings of William E. McLellin," *The Latter-day Saints' Millennial Star* 26 (1864), 808.

13. "History and Writings of William E. McLellin," *The Latter-day Saints' Millennial Star.*

M. Hinkle, William Law, Sidney Rigdon, James J. Strang, David Whitmer, and Granville Hedrick before leaving organized religion altogether in 1869.[14] He died in Independence, Jackson County, Missouri, on March 14, 1883.[15]

LAUNCHING A MAGNIFICENT MISSIONARY LABOR: DOCTRINE AND COVENANTS 65

On 30 October 1831, just one day after Doctrine and Covenants section 66 was revealed, the Prophet received another revelation, now recorded in section 65, which contains significant doctrinal insights into the Lord's command to "go forth to proclaim my gospel" (Doctrine and Covenants 75:2). Earlier that year the Lord had launched a significant missionary endeavor by the Church originating from Kirtland. In fact, the Lord commanded the New York Saints to "go to the Ohio" because "there I will give unto you my law" and "from thence, whosoever I will shall go forth among all nations (Doctrine and Covenants 38:32–33).

Just a few days after the Prophet arrived in Kirtland, the Lord began to fulfill some of the promises made in that revelation. He instructed twelve elders to "hearken and hear and obey the law which I shall give unto you" (Doctrine and Covenants 42:3), then revealed the "first commandment" (verse 4) in His, law saying that those elders and many more after them "shall go forth in the power of my Spirit, preaching my gospel, two by two, in my name" (verse 6).

He continued his focus on missionary work in thirteen of the next twenty-two sections recorded in the Doctrine and Covenants prior to the Prophet's move to Hiram, including the five while the Prophet and others were in Missouri. In these revelations, as shown in Table 1, he gave a general command to preach in five sections, called specific brethren to preach in seven sections, promised blessings for preaching

14. Porter, Larry C. "The Odyssey of William Earl McLellin: Man of Diversity, 1806–83." In *The Journals of William E. McLellin, 1831–1836,* edited by Jan Shipps and John W. Welch, (Provo, UT: BYU Studies; Urbana: University of Illinois Press, 1994), 291–378.
15. findagrave.com/memorial/10277.

in three, specified where and/or to whom in nine, directed how to teach in five, and explained what to teach in seven sections.

Table 1: Selected Doctrine and Covenants Passages Relating to Missionary Work

Type of Direction Related to Missionary Work	Citations
General command	49:26; 57:10; 58:64; 63:37, 57
Specific brethren called	50:37–38; 52:3, 7, 8, 22, 23, 24, 25, 26, 27, 28–32, 35, 37, 39; 53:1; 55:1; 58:61; 60:6, 8; 61:30–32, 33
Promised blessings	49:5, 26; 52:34; 61:34
Where, when, to whom to preach	43:20; 44:3; 45:64; 45:1; 49:1–3; 52:3, 7, 8, 22, 23, 25, 26, 27, 33, 35, 36, 39; 58:46, 47; 60:6, 8; 61:30–32, 33
How to teach	43:15; 52:9, 10, 22, 23, 25, 26, 27; 58:63; 60:7, 13–14; 61:3
What to teach	43:20; 45:64; 49:4, 11–14; 52:9, 36; 53:3; 55:1; 58:7–13, 63

It was quite common for individuals to be called on several short-term missions lasting just a few months, many of them during the winter months when there was less farm work to be done. Orson Hyde described the conditions accompanying one of their missions, typical of the time of no "purse or scrip" (Doctrine and Covenants 24:18):

> To travel two thousand miles on foot, teaching from house to house, and from city to city, without purse or scrip, often sleeping in school houses after preaching—in barns, in sheds, by the way side, under trees, &c., was something of a task. When one would be teaching in private families, the other would frequently be nodding in his chair, weary with toil, fatigue and want of sleep. We were often rejected in the after part of the day, compelling us to travel in the evening, and sometimes till people were gone to bed, leaving us to lodge where we could. We would sometimes travel until midnight or until nearly daylight before we would find a barn or shed in which we dare to lie down; must be away before discovered least suspicion rest upon us. Would often lie down under trees and sleep in daytime to make up loss.[16]

Brigham Young also added, "Many times I have walked till my feet were sore and the blood would run in my shoes and out of them, and fill my appointments—go into houses, ask for something to eat, sing and talk to them and when they would commence questioning, answering them."[17]

Due to Joseph's and Sidney's previous missionary labors along with those of other missionaries who had followed, there may have been as many as one hundred Church members in the Hiram area by this time.[18] In addition to a branch in Hiram, another was organized in nearby Nelson, followed soon by branches in Mantua and Shalersville. Joseph would have probably preached in these branches on at least some of the six Sundays that followed his arrival, as was his custom.

On the seventh Sunday, 30 October 1831, members of the Hiram Branch and possibly other investigators gathered at the Johnson Home

---

16. "History of Orson Hyde," *Millennial Star* 26 (1864), 776.
17. Brigham Young, *Journal of Discourses* 13 (January 2, 1870), 89.
18. Levi Jackman, *A Short Sketch of Life, 1851.* ca. 1851. Typescript. CHL. M270.1 J123ja 18—?.

to worship. During the meeting, William McLellin spoke for an hour and a half, later recalling, "And it was not I but the spirit and power of God which was in me."[19] Then in the presence of those attending the meeting, Joseph received a revelation now known as Doctrine and Covenants 65.

The Prophet introduced this revelation saying, "In the fore part of October, I received the following prayer through revelation."[20] Alluding to Daniel's prophecy, this revelation indicated that because "keys of the kingdom of God are committed unto man on the earth from thence shall the gospel roll forth unto the ends of the earth . . . that his kingdom may go forth upon the earth, that the inhabitants thereof may receive it, and be prepared for the days to come, in the which the Son of Man shall acome down in heaven" (verses 2 and 5). Regarding this prophecy, the Prophet later stated: "I calculate to be one of the instruments of setting up the kingdom of Daniel by the word of the Lord, and I intend to lay a foundation that will revolutionize the whole world."[21]

MISSION CALLS OF EDEN SMITH, STEPHEN BURNETT, JARED CARTER, AND JOHN MURDOCK

Four sections of the Doctrine and Covenants are treated in this chapter—75, 79, 80, and 99—because they exemplify the role of revelation in the calling, assigning to a field of labor, and the naming of companionships. Sections 79, 80, and 99 were revealed in Hiram. Section 75 was revealed in Amherst, Ohio, but because the revelation occurred while Joseph and Emma maintained the Johnsons' home as a residence, it is included in this volume.

---

19. Jan Shipps and John W. Welch, eds., *The Journals of William E. McLellin, 1831–1836* (Provo, UT: BYU Studies; Urbana, IL: University of Illinois Press, 1994), 45.

20. History, 1838–1856, Volume A-1 [23 December 1805–30 August 1834], 153, *The Joseph Smith Papers*, josephsmithpapers.org/paper-summary/history-1838–1856–volume-a-1–23–december-1805–30–august-1834/1

21. History, 1838–1856, volume F-1 [1 May 1844–8 August 1844] 18, *The Joseph Smith Papers*, josephsmithpapers.org/paper-summary/history-1838–1856–volume-f-1-1–may-1844–8–august-1844/1

On 25 January 1831, approximately two weeks after the Prophet and Sidney Rigdon were directed in section 73 to return to their translation work, the Prophet held a conference in Amherst, Ohio, fifty miles west of Kirtland of which, the Prophet wrote, "Much harmony prevailed, and considerable business was done to advance the kingdom, and promulgate the Gospel to the inhabitants of the surrounding country. The Elders seemed anxious for me to inquire of the Lord that they might know His will, or learn what would be most pleasing to Him for them to do, in order to bring men to a sense of their condition."[22] The elders' desires were realized when two revelations were given during the conference calling twenty-four brethren on missions—ten brethren initially and then fourteen more who had "given [their] names that [they] might know his will concerning [them]" (verse 23). The initial ten received their call, and an assignment to a field of labor and to a companion. The other fourteen also received calls and companion assignments, but the Lord said they could go any direction "to the east or to the west, or to the north, or to the south" (verse 26).

These two revelations were combined and are now known as section 75. Besides the revelations, the conference saw the appointment of Orson Pratt to serve as elders president and the sustaining and ordaining of Joseph as president of the high priesthood by Sidney Rigdon, an act that represents an important step in establishing the First Presidency. (Note section 74 is not discussed in this book. It was revealed in New York in 1830 and thus is not associated with the Kirtland and Hiram period of the Church.) Three months later, on 7 March 1832, section 80 was received and directed specifically to Stephen Burnett and Eden Smith. In his history, the Prophet introduced it along with three other sections that precede or follow it chronologically—78, 79, and 81—by referring to the work of translation and that he had "received the four following revelations."[23]

---

22. History of the Church 1:242–243.
23. Ibid., 1:255.

At the Amherst conference, these brethren had been called by the Lord to serve as missionaries and were assigned other companions (see D&C 75:35–36). In section 80, the Lord changed the pairings and assigned them to work together. Later that fall, two weeks prior to Joseph Smith's move back to Kirtland from Hiram on September 12, 1832, the Lord revealed section 99 to John Murdock, who as a widower left his children in the care of other families for over a year while he served.

The Four Missionaries

Stephen Burnett was from Orange, Ohio, and joined the Church in November 1830 at the age of seventeen. He was taught the gospel by John Murdock, who had been one of the early converts baptized when the first missionaries came to Ohio. The Burnett family hosted the October 1831 conference in their home at which attended most, if not all, of the twelve brethren who had seen the Book of Mormon plates. This conference was also the second time high priests were ordained in this dispensation (the first time was the June 1831 conference on the Isaac and Lucy Morley farm), and interestingly, seventeen–year-old Stephen was one of them.

Later Stephen served other missions to New Hampshire in 1832–1834 and was president of the Bath New Hampshire Conference. In 1837, he engaged in a debate with a Campbellite leader, William Haydon, and exchanged letters with him, demonstrating a great degree of commitment to the Prophet and to the Restoration. Ironically, he left the Church the same year and then in 1853 joined the Campbellites himself and became an elder in that organization.

Eden Smith was born in Indiana in 1806, the son of John Smith (not the Prophet's uncle) and became a resident at some point of the Northampton Township in Summit County, Ohio, 200 miles from Kirtland. Eden was called to "go ye and preach my gospel" (Doctrine and Covenants 80:3) and in response to this and other calls his journal records a number of short missions in Summit, Wayne, Medina, Portage, and Stark counties, Ohio. Following his mission in April 1832, Eden moved his family to be near his father in Chippewa, Ohio, which is sixty miles south of Kirtland. The records state that his father received Church discipline around July 1833 but was not excommunicated despite being unrepentant and critical of Church leadership. Eden was also apparently excommunicated around that time because William E. McLellin's journal indicates that he rebaptized Eden in 1834. There is little else recorded about his life other than in 1842 he moved to Nauvoo, served in the Nauvoo Legion, and was called on a mission to Pennsylvania in 1843. He must have traveled from Nauvoo with the Saints because the record shows that in 1848 he was residing in Pottawattamie County, Iowa, the Iowa side of the Winter Quarters area. He returned to Indiana and died in 1851.

Jared Carter was baptized in Colesville, New York, and traveled with the Colesville Branch to Kirtland in the spring of 1831, settled with them in Thompson, but did not accompany them to Missouri. He served three missions in 1832–33 and was ordained a high priest in 1833. He was a member of the Kirtland Temple building committee in 1833 and later labored on the temple in 1835. He served a fourth mission in northern Canada and was appointed a member of the Kirtland High Council in 1834 and president of the council in 1837. Jared moved his family with the Saints to Far West, Missouri, where he again served on the high council, then moved again to Nauvoo. Following the death of the Prophet, he temporarily associated with James J. Strang's organization, then returned to the Church. He died at the age of forty-eight in DeKalb County, Illinois.[24]

John Murdock's record of missionary service was extraordinary. He had been a Reformed Baptist preacher, was baptized by Parley P. Pratt as one of the early Ohio converts, and immediately began preaching the gospel for the next four months during which time he baptized seventy people and established the Orange and Warrensville branches. His wife, Julia, died giving birth to twins the same day the Prophet and Emma lost their twins, resulting in his twins' adoption

---

24. Carter, Jared (Biography), *The Joseph Smith Papers*, 16 November 2019, josephsmithpapers.org/person/jared-carter

by the Smiths. Up to the time he joined Zion's Camp in 1834, he had been gone from home most of the time serving missions. He served a total of thirteen missions in all, including one to Australia,[25] as well as on two high councils, as a bishop in Nauvoo and Salt Lake City, and as a patriarch.

---

25. Murdock, John (Biography), *The Joseph Smith Papers*, 16 November 2019, josephsmithpapers.org/person/john-murdock.

CHRONOLOGICAL SUMMARY

12 Sept. 1831:   Joseph, Emma, and family arrive at Johnson Home

26 Sept. 1831:   JST recommenced by this date in Hiram

25–26 Oct. 1831: Conference in Orange, Ohio

29 Oct. 1831:   William E. McLellin's five questions (section 66)

30 Oct. 1831:   Keys of the Kingdom (section 65)

1–12 Nov. 1831: Several conferences—publishing revelations

1 Dec. 1831:   JST postponed for dealing with apostates (section 71)

Chapter 6

"The Voice of the Lord Is Unto All Men"

An Introduction to the Revelations Received During the November 1831 Conferences

Reflecting on his experience as a revelator, Joseph Smith wrote, "It is my meditation all the day, and more than my meat and drink, to know how I shall make the Saints of God comprehend the visions that roll like an overflowing surge before my mind. . . . Hosanna, hosanna, hosanna to Almighty God, that rays of light begin to burst forth upon us even now."[1]

PREPARATIONS FOR PRINTING

Joseph was constantly receiving revelation, and from the day the Church was first organized the Lord instructed that "there shall be a record kept among you" (Doctrine and Covenants 21:1) so that the revelations could be collected and shared. Three months later, the voice of the Lord again told the Prophet to "continue in calling upon God in my name, and writing the things which shall be given thee by

---

1. Joseph Smith, "Chapter 45: Joseph Smith's Feelings about His Prophetic Mission," *Teachings of Presidents of the Church: Joseph Smith,* (2011), lds.org/manual/teachings-joseph-smith/chapter-45?lang=eng

the Comforter" (Doctrine and Covenants 24:5). Early records suggest that the Prophet's first revelations were recorded on loose pages and stored together. Some of these were sewn together, as were the Book of Mormon manuscripts.[2]

From the time of the formal organization of the Church in 1830 until November 1831, obtaining a copy of the Prophet's revelations required traveling to Joseph's home and copying them by hand or copying someone else's copy. Orson Pratt recalled, "We often had access to the manuscripts [of the revelations] when boarding with the Prophet; and it was our delight to read them over and over again, before they were printed. And so highly were they esteemed by us, that we committed some to memory; and a few we copied for the purpose of reference in our absence on missions; and also to read them to the saints for their edification."[3] However, copying by hand was time-consuming and resulted in numerous errors in the copies—everything from simple omissions or word changes to the adding of actual content.

As early as June of 1830, while living in Harmony, Pennsylvania, Joseph, with the assistance of John Whitmer, began compiling his revelations, anticipating their eventual publication. Before specific plans were made to publish them, Joseph had received revelations that would later be recorded in the Doctrine and Covenants, thirty-eight of which were received after the compilation began.

Two revelations, which now constitute sections 55 and 57, were directed toward William W. Phelps, a printer from New York, as the Lord prepared for eventually publishing the revelations. Before being baptized, William and his family traveled to Kirtland in June 1831, and arrived about a week after the June conference, during which several brethren were directed to travel to Jackson County, Missouri. On the day of the Phelps family's arrival, Joseph sought the Lord's will concerning William, and the Lord revealed that he should be baptized and receive the Holy Ghost, then be ordained "by my servant

---

2. Robin Scott Jensen, "A Bit of Old String: Mary Whitmer's Unheralded Contributions," *Treasures of the Collection*, history.lds.org/article/mary-whitmer-book-of-mormon?lang=eng

3. Orson Pratt, "Explanation of Names in the Covenants," *The Seer* 2 (March, 1854), 228.

Joseph Smith, Jun." (Doctrine and Covenants 55:2). He then directed that William "be ordained to assist . . . Oliver Cowdery to do the work of printing" and take his "journey" to Missouri (Doctrine and Covenants 55:4–5).

In the first revelation received in Missouri, the Lord directed that "William be planted in this place, and be established as a printer unto the church" (Doctrine and Covenants 57:11). He then reversed the roles William and Oliver fulfilled when He said, "And let my servant Oliver Cowdery assist him" (Doctrine and Covenants 57:11, 13). In the fall William traveled back to Kirtland to retrieve his family and acquire printing supplies, then stopped in Cincinnati, Ohio, on his return to Missouri to acquire the Church's first printing press and type. Thus, the way was prepared for the printing of Joseph's revelations in Missouri, the Book of Commandments.

The Book of Commandments continued a pattern of record-keeping and publication. The Book of Mormon was first recorded on handwritten, foolscap paper, copied by hand as a printer's manuscript, and printed as a first edition in 1829 and 1830 by E. B. Grandin. Commencing on the day the Church was organized, Oliver Cowdery served as the first Church recorder. By June 1830 Joseph began collecting and organizing his revelations, and by August he and his scribes had also recorded forty-six pages of a Bible revision manuscript. In 1831 they began a handwritten record called *The Book of Commandments and Revelations.* In 1832 five different record-keeping projects commenced: in February or March the *Kirtland Revelation Book*, during the summer the *History of Joseph Smith*, in the fall a gathering of loose letters received during the previous three years as the Prophet's first letterbook and also a journal, and in December a minute book later known as the *Kirtland Council Minute Book.*

REVELATIONS AT FOUR CONFERENCES IN TWELVE DAYS

Shortly before November, Joseph and other Church leaders had likely made the decision to publish this compilation and selected a name for it—the Book of Commandments. The timing of the decision may have been affected by difficulties following publication in a local newspaper of nine letters written by Ezra Booth criticizing Joseph Smith and the Church.

The first day of November began a remarkable twelve-day period in which four conferences were held in the Johnsons' home: 1–2, 3, 8–9, and 11–12 November. Joseph had gathered some ten leading brethren to "conference" (counsel) together regarding the publication of about seventy revelations that had been received by this time—Oliver Cowdery, John, David, Christian, and Peter Whitmer Jr., Sidney Rigdon, Luke and Lyman Johnson, Orson Hyde, and William E. McLellin. Although some revelatory events may have included preaching, most conferences resembled what later became known in the Church as a council. The brethren gathered in the "revelation room," John and Elsa's former bedroom that served as an office. Ironically, during the seven days of conferences when the brethren had gathered to discuss publication of the revelations, Joseph received eight additional revelations.

Despite the efforts of John Whitmer and others, the exact chronology of the events during the twelve-day period, especially the first two days, is not known. The timing of some of these events is well documented (Minute Book 1), but not others. Therefore, various historians and writers have provided their own conjectured chronologies, including the one shown in the following table representing our research. (A summary of the events of the conferences is provided here, and more detailed portrayals appear in subsequent chapters.)

TABLE 1: EARLY NOVEMBER REVELATIONS

Date	Conference Number	Topic(s)	D&C Section
1 November	1	Specific instructions to four brethren; literal descendants of Aaron as bishops; parental duties	68

1 November	1	The Lord's Preface to His "Book of . . . Commandments"	1
2 November	1	The Lord's response to those who challenged the language of the revelations	67
2 November	1	Testimony of witnesses to the Book of the Lord's Commandments	Introduction
3 November	2	The Lord's Appendix	133
8 November	3	Conference decision for Joseph to correct scribal errors	unpublished
11 November	4	Instruction for John Whitmer to accompany Oliver Cowdery in transporting *The Book of the Lord's Commandments* to Missouri	69
11 November	4	Revelation on the priesthood	Latter portion of 107
12 November	4	"Literary firm" established to finance and financially benefit from *The Book of the Lord's Commandments* publication	70

PRINTING DECISIONS

On the morning of 1 November, the conference began with Oliver Cowdery requesting that the conference determine "the mind of the Lord" as to how many copies to print.[4] The conference boldly decided to publish 10,000 copies—twice the number of the first edition Book of Mormon—which suggests they recognized the role the book would play in the Restoration. By comparison, the 1830 publication of the Book of Mormon was a very large print run for any press, but especially for one of its size located in a rural community. The usual number of book copies produced during that time ranged from 500 to 1,000, and surpassing 2,000 copies was rare, even in the publication centers of Boston, Philadelphia, and New York. The optimistic decision to print 10,000 copies, therefore, was extraordinary.

April 1832 saw the decision to reduce the publication size to 3,000, probably due to the extremely high cost of purchasing large amounts of paper, which was in short supply. Printing at this time involved printing signatures, large sheets of papers with multiple pages that would be folded to form a book, then collecting the folded sheets into a "gathering." If printing the book would require six gatherings, a print run of 10,000 copies would require sixty reams of paper, while 3,000 copies would require only eighteen reams.[5]

A PREFACE AND A WITNESS STATEMENT

Either before or following the decision regarding the number of copies to be printed, the revelation given for Orson, Luke, Lyman, and William, later known as section 68, was probably revealed.[6]

---

4. Robin Scott Jensen, "From Manuscript to Printed Page: An Analysis of the History of the Book of Commandments and Revelations," *BYU Studies* 48(3).

5. Book of Commandments, "1833: Historical Introduction," *The Joseph Smith Papers*, josephsmithpapers.org/paper-summary/book-of-commandments-1833/189#historical-intro

6. Book of Commandments, 1833: Historical Introduction, *The Joseph Smith Papers*.

Not satisfied with the attempts of Sidney, Oliver, and William to write a preface to the Book of Commandments after the conference began, the other brethren asked the Prophet to seek a revelation. He led the conference in prayer, to which the Lord responded with His own preface, which later became section 1 of the Doctrine and Covenants. Joseph then testified of the great blessing publishing the Lord's revelations would be and asked the brethren if they were willing to bear testimony of the truthfulness of this book to all the world, much like the three and eight witnesses of the Book of Mormon. A number of the brethren arose and said that they were willing to testify to the world that they knew that they were of the Lord.[7] A written testimony was revealed, and the following day's sessions began with Oliver Cowdery reading it to the brethren.

LANGUAGE AND TRANSPORTATION ISSUES

It was probably at that point that some of the brethren expressed concerns about the language of the revelations and were hesitant to affix their names to the testimony. The Lord then gave the revelation that later became section 67 of the Doctrine and Covenants, which challenged the "wisest" among the brethren to see if one or more of them could write any of the revelations with language superior to the Prophet's. William McLellin accepted the challenge and failed "miserably." The reluctant brethren humbled themselves and expressed a willingness to testify.[8]

At a second conference, held on the 3 November, the appendix to the Book of Commandments was revealed. The brethren decided "that Elder Oliver Cowdery should carry the commandments and revelations to Independence, Missouri, for printing, and that I [Joseph Smith] should arrange and get them in readiness by the

---

7. Minutes, 1–2 November 1831, *The Joseph Smith Papers*, josephsmithpapers. org/paper-summary/minutes-1–2–november-1831/2.

8. History, 1838–1856, volume A-1 [23 December 1805–30 August 1834], 162, *The Joseph Smith Papers,* josephsmithpapers.org/paper-summary/ history-1838–1856–volume-a-1–23–december-1805–30–august-1834/168

time that he left, which was to be by—or, if possible, before—the 15th of the month"[9]

During the third conference, on 8 and 9 November, Joseph was assigned to correct "those errors or mistakes which he may discover by the holy Spirit."[10] Some of the revisions in the *Book of Commandments and Revelations* appear in his handwriting along with Sidney Rigdon's. Other revisions were made by Oliver Cowdery and John Whitmer, all or some of which may have been made prior to transporting the book to Missouri for printing. Later in Missouri William W. Phelps also contributed some revising relating to much of the punctuation and versification along with many of the other copy editing changes. He made few alterations in the original language.

The fourth conference, on 11 and 12 November, began with the revelation later designated as section 69, which directed John Whitmer to accompany Oliver Cowdery in transporting the manuscript of the revelations to Missouri, along with another revelation relating to Church government, later comprising about one-half of section 107. On 12 November, Joseph and some of these other brethren were commanded to form a "literary firm" (section 70) and charged with overseeing the printing of the Book of Commandments and numerous other printing projects—two newspapers, an almanac, and a hymnal—although printing the latter two was not accomplished until much later.

PROCESSES OF REVELATION

As revelations were so abundant and so significant during this period, some understanding of the manner in which Joseph generally received revelation is relevant. Subsequent chapters include detailed discussions of the eight revelations of this conference.

The Prophet received guidance from the Lord in various ways, including visions, divine appearances, angelic visitations, audible

---

9. History, 1838–1856, volume A-1 [23 December 1805–30 August 1834], 166, *The Joseph Smith Papers*.

10. Minutes, 8 November 1831, *The Joseph Smith Papers*, 24 November 2018, josephsmithpapers.org/paper-summary/minutes-8–november-1831/1.

voices, and spiritual impressions that "roll[ed] like an overflow-ing surge before [his] mind."[11] As with the Book of Mormon translation, he never detailed how he received revelations from God, even when asked about it publicly. Fortunately scribes and other observers were often present when the Lord spoke with and through Joseph, some of whom provided details about what they saw, heard, and felt.

Some commented on his appearance during times of revelation. Brigham Young indicated that Joseph was often transfigured when receiving revelation as he preached or taught under the guidance of the Spirit. "Those who were acquainted with him knew when the Spirit of revelation was upon him, for his countenance wore an expres-sion peculiar to himself while under that influence. He preached by the Spirit of revelation, and taught in his council by it, and those who were acquainted with him could discover it at once, for at such times there was a peculiar clearness and transparency in his face."[12]

Jared Carter and Ebenezer Page met with the Prophet prior to leaving for a mission in Vermont. Later, in September 1832, Jared recalled: "In the afternoon we had a meeting and Brother Joseph, the prophet & seer, before the meeting closed had the spirit of prophecy come on him while he was looking upon me and I saw that the form of his countenance was changed."[13]

The most common means of revelatory communication involved Joseph giving words to the spiritual impressions upon his mind. As Orson Pratt explained, "Joseph . . . received the ideas from God, but clothed those ideas with such words as came to his mind."[14] The Lord had trained the Prophet to engage in this type of experience through the process of translating the Book of Mormon, initially scaffolded

---

11. Joseph Smith, "Chapter 45: Joseph Smith's Feelings about His Prophetic Mission."

12. Brigham Young, "Priesthood," *Journal of Discourses* 9, (May 7, 1861), 89.

13. Carter, J. (Sept. 1832). *Journal*, MS 1441, Church History Library, The Church of Jesus Christ of Latter-day Saints, 6.

14. Orson Pratt, *Minutes of the School of the Prophets*, Salt Lake Stake, Dec. 9, 1872, Church History Library, The Church of Jesus Christ of Latter-day Saints, as quoted in Robert J. Woodford, "The Story of the Doctrine and Covenants," *Ensign* (December 1984), 32.

by the Urim and Thummim and a seer stone but later performed independent of such devices. Commenting on the Book of Mormon translation, Orson Pratt said, "Joseph Smith told him that he used the Urim and Thummim when he was inexperienced at translation but that later he did not need it, which was the case in Joseph's translation of many verses of the Bible" (see also chapter 3).[15]

Scribes and others who witnessed the process were impressed with the fluency with which the Prophet dictated the revelations. Parley P. Pratt related this observation when section 50 was revealed on the Morley farm:

> Each sentence was uttered slowly and very distinctly, and with a pause between each, sufficiently long for it to be recorded, by an ordinary writer, in long hand. This was the manner in which all his written revelations were dictated and written. There was never any hesitation, reviewing, or reading back in order to keep the run of the subject; neither did any of these communications undergo revisions, interlinings, or corrections. As he dictated them so they stood, so far as I have witnessed; and I was present to witness the dictation of several communications of several pages each.[16]

William E. McLellin wrote similarly:

> The scribe seats himself at a desk or table, with pen, ink and paper. The subject of enquiry being understood, the Prophet and Revelator enquires of God. He spiritually sees, hears and feels, and then speaks as he is moved upon by the Holy Ghost, the "thus saith the Lord," sentence after sentence, and waits for his (scribe) to write and then read aloud each sentence. Thus they proceed until the revelator says Amen, at the close of what is then communicated. I have known [prophets] to seat themselves, & without premeditation . . . thus deliver off in broken sentences, some of the most sublime pieces of composition which I ever perused in any book.[17]

---

15. Neal A. Maxwell, "By the Gift and Power of God, *Ensign* (Janaury 1997), lds. org/ensign/1997/01/by-the-gift-and-power-of-god?lang=eng
16. Parley Parker Pratt, *The Autobiography of Parley Parker Pratt,* ed. Parley P. Pratt (Chicago: Law, King & Law, 1874), 65–66.
17. Jan Shipps and John W. Welch, eds., *The Journals of William E. McLellin, 1831–1836* (Provo, UT: BYU Studies; Urbana IL: University of Illinois Press, 1994), 51.

The Lord did not expect the Prophet to be instantaneously perfect at receiving and recording His words. To give voice to His words He had chosen a mortal who was subject to weaknesses and imperfections. "[T]hese commandments are of me, and were given unto my servants in their weakness, after the manner of their language" (Doctrine and Covenants 1:24). Joseph himself lamented: "I cannot find words in which to express myself. I am not learned, but I have as good feelings as any man. Oh, that I had the language of the archangel to express my feelings once to my friends! But I never expect to in this life."[18]

In addition to the challenge posed by his literary weaknesses, Joseph belied the imperfections inherent in English—a "crooked, broken, scattered, and imperfect language."[19] Joseph needed to edit the revelations to adjust punctuation and grammar, change or add words to clarify intended meaning, combine multiple revelations, and adjust language as additional doctrinal and procedural insights were revealed to him. None of these revisions, however, involved correcting errors in the fundamental substance of the revelations.[20] As Joseph later explained, "I never told you I was perfect; but there is no error in the revelations which I have taught."[21] Similarly, the Lord himself stated, "There is no unrighteousness in them" (Doctrine and Covenants 67:9). Much of this inspired work of revising occurred in one of three contexts: when the revelations were first dictated, when they were recopied from original records to relatively more "permanent" records such as *The Book of Commandments and Revelations*, and when they were being prepared for publication.

---

18. Joseph Smith, *Teachings of Presidents of the Church: Joseph Smith* (Salt Lake City, UT: The Church of Jesus Christ of Latter-day Saints, 2007), 520.

19. Joseph Smith to William W. Phelps, Nov. 27, 1832, in *Personal Writings of Joseph Smith*, ed. Dean C. Jessee (Salt Lake City, UT: Deseret Book Company, 1984), 262.

20. Marlin K. Jensen, "The Joseph Smith Papers: The Manuscript Revelation Books," *Ensign* (July 2009), 46–51.

21. Minute Book 2, *The Joseph Smith Papers*, josephsmithpapers.org/paper -summary/minute-book-2/20

These frequent, yet miraculous revelatory experiences laid the doctrinal and organizational foundation for the Church. As mentioned, an overwhelming amount of revelation was received during the twelve days of conferences that involved plans for printing the revelations Joseph had received up to November 1831. Those eight revelations were added to the book then known as the Book of Commandments, later published as the Doctrine and Covenants.

As the 1831 conference participants declared, this "book of Revelation" to be published would be "the foundation of the Church & the salvation of the world & the Keys of the mysteries of the Kingdom & the riches of Eternity to the Church." The notice of the publication in the Church newspaper stated its purpose was that the Church "may lift up their heads and rejoice, and praise his holy name, that they are permitted to live in the days when he returns to his people his everlasting covenant, to prepare them for his Presence."[22]

The earliest publication venue for the revelations was *The Evening and Morning Star,* which began publication in Missouri in June 1832, "devoted to the revelations of God as made known to his servants by the Holy Ghost, at sundry times since the creation of man, but more especially in these last days."[23] Unfortunately, the Church was going to have to wait nearly four years in order to enjoy a compiled publication of the revelations. The revelations were transported in late 1831 to Missouri where the Church press was located, and initial publication work resulted in publication of many of them in the Church periodical, *The Evening and Morning Star.* The publication of the actual Book of Commandments did not commence until the summer of 1833 and was left incomplete when an angry mob destroyed the press and drove the Saints out of Jackson County. Only about one hundred copies of the partially completed book survived. It was not until 1835 when the first edition of the Doctrine

---

22. "Revelations," *The Evening and the Morning Star,* 1(12) (May 1833), 89.
23. Revelations printed in *The Evening and the Morning Star,* June 1832–June 1833, "Source Note," *The Joseph Smith Papers,* josephsmithpapers.org/paper-summary/revelations-printed-in-the-evening-and-the-morning-star-june-1832–june-1833/1#historical-intro.

and Covenants was printed that the revelations were available for use by the general Church. Describing the Book of Commandments and all editions of the Doctrine and Covenants, the introduction to the current edition says it is "unique because it is not a translation of an ancient document, but is of modern origin and was given of God through His chosen prophets for the restoration of His holy work and the establishment of the kingdom of God on the earth in these days. In the revelations, one hears the tender but firm voice of the Lord Jesus Christ, speaking anew in the dispensation of the fulness of times; and the work that is initiated (within its pages) is preparatory to His Second Coming, in fulfillment of and in concert with the words of all the holy prophets since the world began."

CHRONOLOGICAL SUMMARY

29 Oct. 1831:   William E. McLellin's five questions (section 66)

30 Oct. 30 1831: Keys of the kingdom (section 65)

1 Nov. 1831:   Four brethren (first of 4 conferences Nov. 11–12; section 68)

1 Nov. 1831:   Preface to Book of the Lord's Commandments (section 1)

1 Nov. 1831:   Challenge to Prophet's revelatory language (section 67)

1 Nov. 1831:   Appendix (second conference; section 133)

1 Nov. 1831:   Dealing with revisions (third conference)

1 Nov. 1831:   John Whitmer to travel to Missouri (fourth conference; section 69)

1 Nov. 1831:   Church government (section 107; 29 verses)

2 Nov. 1831:   Intro recording witnesses' testimony

3 Nov. 1831:   Appendix (section 133)

8–9 Nov. 1831: Brethren deal with revisions

11 Nov. 1831:   John Whitmer to travel to Missouri (section 69)

11 Nov. 1831:   Instructions on Church government (section 107)

12 Nov. 1831:   The Litserary Firm (section 70)

Chapter 7

"What I the Lord Have Spoken"

November Conferences:
Doctrine and Covenants 68, 1, 67, and 133

Luke Johnson was baptized by Joseph Smith on 10 May 1831, two months after Lyman and his parents. Luke served his first mission in southern Ohio shortly after his baptism. On his second mission, which was to Virginia about a year later, he married Susan Harminda Poteet on 1 November 1833,[1] and they lived first on his parents' farm. Luke later served several missions throughout Ohio, Pennsylvania, Virginia, Kentucky, New York, and Canada. He ran the family farm for a short time in 1833, then moved to Kirtland with many of the active Saints from Hiram. A year later he was appointed a member of the Kirtland High Council, participated in Zion's Camp, and was called and ordained an Apostle on 15 February 1835. (A table specifying ordination information for the original Twelve Apostles appears in the appendix to this book.)

Unfortunately, after two years of faithful service as an Apostle, Luke became embroiled in the difficulties associated with the collapse of the Kirtland Safety Society during the nationwide Panic of 1837, and his faith in Joseph Smith and the restored gospel waned. "Having

---

1. Luke Johnson, *The Joseph Smith Papers*, josephsmithpapers.org/person/luke-johnson.

partaken of the spirit of speculation, which at that time was possessed by many of the Saints and Elders, my mind became darkened, and I was left to pursue my own course. I lost the Spirit of God, and neglected my duty; the consequence was, that at a conference held in Kirtland, Sept. 3rd, 1837, in company with my brother Lyman and John F. Boynton, I was cut off from the Church."[2]

These three, along with Orson Pratt and William W. Phelps, swore out charges against the Prophet and Sidney Rigdon in May of 1837. In consequence they were disfellowshipped and dropped from the Quorum of the Twelve on 3 September 1837, then reinstated a week later by the Kirtland High Council.[3] (Orson soon repented, but William continued his fight against the Church.[4]) In October, Luke and Lyman were disfellowshipped for participating in a dance where "our young brethren and sisters [were] mingling themselves with the world."[5] Eventually all three men were excommunicated from the Church in April 1838 by a council in Far West, Missouri.[6] During this period of disaffection Luke seemed to have remained friendly with the Saints. Although the historical records suggest somewhat different dates,[7] it appears that while serving as the Kirtland constable he saved both the Prophet and Joseph Sr. from improper legal action.

Luke did not leave Kirtland along with most of the Saints in 1838, but rather took his family to Virginia, where he studied medicine for a year and then returned to Kirtland to practice. In 1846 he took his family to Nauvoo to join with the Saints as they migrated west. In a

---

2. Luke S. Johnson, "History of Luke Johnson," *Millennial Star*, Jan. 7, 1865.

3. Minute Book 1, 10 Sept. 1837, The Joseph Smith Papers, 26 November 2018, josephsmithpapers.org/paper-summary/minute-book-1/245

4. William McLellin's activities included joining others in swearing out an affidavit against the saints leading to the infamous "Extermination Order" signed by Governor Liburn W. Boggs, the incarceration of the Prophet and others in Liberty Jail, and the expulsion of the saints from Missouri.

5. Andrew Jenson, "Johnson, Luke S.," *LDS Biographical Encyclopedia I* (Salt Lake City: Andrew Jenson History Co., 1901, 86).

6. Kirtland Township Trustee Minutes, 1817–1846, May 7, 1838 as found in Mark L. Staker, *Hearken O Ye People: The Historical Setting for Joseph Smith's Ohio Revelations.* (Salt Lake City, UT: Greg Kofford Books, 2009, 387).

7. Lawrence R. Flake, *Prophets and Apostles of the Last Dispensation* (Provo, UT: Religious Studies Center, Brigham Young University, 2001), 363–365.

meeting of the Saints, his brother-in-law, Orson Hyde, introduced him to the congregation, and Luke is purported to have said, "I have stopped by the wayside and stood aloof from the work of the Lord. . . . But my heart is with this people. I want to be associated with the saints, go with them into the wilderness and continue with them to the end."[8]

Orson then rebaptized and reconfirmed him, and Luke and his family joined the vanguard company led by Brigham Young that headed west. His wife, Susan, died while the family crossed Iowa, leaving Luke and their six children. He then married America Morgan Clark and continued west with Brigham Young, leaving his family in Kanesville. He returned to Kanesville for his family, then traveled to Utah and settled near Tooele, where he practiced medicine, farmed, and served as a bishop but was never reinstated to the Quorum of the Twelve. At the time of his death, Brigham Young affirmed, "Since his return to the Church he has lived to the truth to the best of his ability and died in the faith."[9]

Lyman Johnson

Lyman was the first member of the Johnson family to join the Church. Like Luke, he traveled widely as a missionary throughout Ohio, the eastern states, and Nova Scotia. In 1834, he participated in Zion's Camp, then married Sarah Susan Long when he returned to Kirtland. On 14 February 1835 he was the first to be ordained an Apostle and was referred to as "great among all the living" with even Satan "trembling before him."[10]

During the days of wild speculation in Kirtland, Lyman and fellow Apostle John F. Boynton invested heavily in land and a store. When the Kirtland Safety Society collapsed, they were left with heavy debts. As mentioned, Lyman received Church discipline along with Luke and John Boynton. Unlike Luke, after his reinstatement he moved his family to Far West, Missouri, where he was later excommunicated.

---

8. B. H. Roberts, *A Comprehensive History of the Church of Jesus Christ of Latter-day Saints* (Provo, UT: Brigham Young University Press, 1965), 5:143.
9. *History of the Church*, 2:188.
10. *Journal of Discourses*, 19:41.

Demonstrating the depths of his apostasy, he joined the Missouri militia in occupying Far West after its surrender.

Unlike Luke, Lyman never fully returned to the Church but did remain loosely connected. He moved to Keokuk, Iowa, across the Mississippi River from Nauvoo, from which he visited the Prophet, former missionary companions, and family members. Lyman married Mary A. (surname unknown) after the death of his first wife and subsequently lived in St. Louis; Chicago; Clarendon, Vermont; then Prairie du Chien, Wisconsin, where he ran a hotel. He died there in a drowning accident at age forty-eight while crossing the partially frozen Mississippi River in 1859. Lyman had previously expressed some regret for leaving the Church he once so faithfully served. Brigham Young recalled hearing Lyman remark, "I would give anything, I would suffer my right hand to be cut off, if I could believe it again. Then I was full of joy and gladness. . . . But now it is darkness, pain, sorrow, misery in the extreme. I have never since seen a happy moment."[11]

Orson Hyde

When Orson was first introduced to the Book of Mormon in Kirtland as a young man, he condemned it as a hoax, but after a year he experienced a change of heart with a determination that he "would never preach against it any more until [he] knew more about it, being pretty strongly convicted in [his] own mind that [he] was doing wrong."[12] He was then baptized and his missionary service began soon after.

Orson's life had its ups and downs, particularly in relation to his Church service. He served a succession of missions after his conversion, taught in the School of the Prophets, represented the Church in Jackson County, Missouri, marched in Zion's Camp, and married Nancy Marinda Johnson, a daughter of John and Elsa Johnson, in Kirtland in September 1834.

On 15 February 1835 Orson was ordained a member of the Quorum of the Twelve Apostles, but was influenced by the disaffection of others in the wake of the society's downfall. He asked for

---

11. *Millennial Star*, 1864, 26:760.
12. *History of the Church*, 3:168.

forgiveness when Heber C. Kimball was preparing for a mission in Great Britain, and asked to accompany Heber. Their work, along with five other brethren in 1837 and 1838, led to the eventual conversion of thousands.

Orson moved with the Kirtland Saints to Far West, Missouri, in the summer of 1838. Once again affected by dissension, he signed an affidavit against the Church in October, although perhaps this occurred under the influence of being "sick with a violent fever."[13] He was temporarily dismissed from the Quorum of the Twelve in May of 1839 but was allowed to return in June 1839. Earlier prophecy had pronounced that Orson was to perform "a great work . . among the Jews,"[14] a prophecy that was fulfilled in 1840 when he was directed to serve a mission that focused on exercising priesthood keys in the gathering of the Jews, and after arriving in Jerusalem, climbed the Mount of Olives and dedicated the holy land.

Orson supervised the completion and dedication of the Nauvoo Temple when the majority of the Saints left for Iowa Territory early in 1846, after which he presided over the British mission. In 1848 he was placed in charge of the "camps of Israel" in the Midwest and remained in Kanesville until 1852. He was later called to preside over the Twelve for twenty-eight years.[15]

SECTION 68: THE OFFICE OF BISHOP

In addition to the calling of these four men to missionary service, section 68 discusses the office of bishop. The gradual revealing of the nature of this office preceded and then continued through the Johnson Home period. Further revelations followed for many years. The history of the appearance of this office in the revelations is instructive. The office of a bishop was first referred to in the "covenants," section 20, but a more careful study of the publication of the Doctrine and Covenants shows that these offices were added to the section as

---

13. *History of the Church*, 4:106.
14. Roy B. Huff, "Orson Hyde: A Life of Lessons Learned," *Religious Educator* 3(2) (2002), 167–183.
15. "Editorial," *The Millennial Star*, 12 June 1852, 14:249, josephsmithpapers.org/person/orson-hyde

the Prophet, acting under inspiration, engaged in preparing the revelations for publication in the first edition.[16]

The Lord highlighted the importance of the office of bishop when he directed that Edward Partridge was to be "ordained to be a bishop" (Doctrine and Covenants 41:9) right after Joseph and Emma arrived in Kirtland in February 1831. He further stressed the bishop's importance by defining the duties of this position in eight additional sections prior to section 68: sections 42, 46, 48, 51, 53, 57, 58, and 64. Section 68 further affirmed the importance of the office by explaining that the highest leadership quorum in the Church, the First Presidency, was to maintain a significant role in appointing, ordaining, designating, and even disciplining bishops. Ten days after section 68 was revealed, the Lord gave additional direction regarding the relationship between the First Presidency (at that time the President of the High Priesthood) and bishops in matters of church discipline Doctrine and Covenants 107).[17]

In obedience to the divine direction to preside "over the Priesthood of Aaron . . . and sit in council with them, to teach them the duties of their office" (Doctrine and Covenants 107:87), both Bishop Partridge and later Bishop Newell K. Whitney organized priest quorums and chose and set apart quorum presidents other than themselves, despite being designated as the presidents of priest quorums in revelation.[22] Bishops functioned similarly to stake officers after the first stakes were created in 1834.

Additional Bishops

On 1 August 1831 the Lord said He had "selected my servant Edward Partridge, and have appointed unto him" (Doctrine and Covenants 58:14) to be bishop in Zion (Jackson County, Missouri) during the time Edward had accompanied Joseph and several other

---

16. Book of Commandments, 1833, The Joseph Smith Papers, josephsmithpapers
.org/paper-summary/book-of-commandments-1833/51#X72D889E7–7C0B
-4CD5–8EF1–EEA5FCBD5265

17. These revelations seem to have been given before a First Presidency had been established, but the title "First Presidency" was included in them at the time the Prophet prepared them for publication in the 1835 edition—see citations in the previous paragraph and chapter 13.

brethren in Missouri. On 1 November 1831, the Lord also directed that "other bishops be set apart unto the church, to minister even according to the first [bishop]"(Doctrine and Covenants 68:14). A month later in Kirtland where the Prophet and other brethren were meeting with leading brethren, the Lord revealed that it was "expedient . . . for a bishop to be appointed . . . in this part of the Lord's vineyard," and "Newel K. Whitney is the man who shall be appointed" (Doctrine and Covenants 72:2, 8). Without directly presiding over any ecclesiastical unit, both bishops oversaw paying bills, purchasing and selling land, undertaking construction projects, printing, and the implementation of the law of consecration in order to care for the needs of the poor, although Edward's responsibility in that regard was more extensive.

The next major revelations directing "other bishops to be set apart" were not given until the Nauvoo period. With the gathering of thousands of Saints in Nauvoo and in two surrounding communities, two stakes were needed in addition to the Nauvoo Stake: one across the Mississippi River in Iowa ("Zarahemla") and the other in Ramus, Illinois. Following the pattern established in Kirtland, each stake had its own presidency, high council, and bishop who continued caring for the poor. Three more bishops were then assigned to serve the needy within Nauvoo's three municipal wards—a designation commonly used to identify political districts in frontier municipalities.[18] The rapid influx of immigrants by August of 1842 led to restructuring those three wards into ten within Nauvoo and three more on the Nauvoo outskirts, each with its own bishop. Like the others, these bishops also did not preside over any ward ecclesiastical organization or congregation because worship and priesthood quorum meetings occurred at a stake or a general Church level; these bishops did, however, organize and lead Aaronic Priesthood quorums.

---

18. William G. Hartley, "Bishop, History of the Office," in *Encyclopedia of Mormonism*, ed. Daniel H. Ludlow (New York City: MacMillan Publishing Company, 1992, 119); Cowdery, William, Jr.," *The Joseph Smith Papers*, josephsmithpapers.org/person/william-cowdery-jr).

"THE LORD'S PREFACE:"
DOCTRINE AND COVENANTS 1

The revelation now known as section 68 of the Doctrine and Covenants occurred during the morning of the first day of the series of conferences. During that morning Oliver Cowdery, William E. McLellin, and Sidney Rigdon were assigned to write a preface for the Book of Commandments, but when their effort was presented to the group it was "picked . . . all to pieces" conference participants "requested Joseph to enquire of the Lord about it" (see also chapter 6).[19] Thus during or immediately after a midday adjournment, the Prophet led the conference in prayer after which he "dictated by the Spirit the preface. . . . Joseph would deliver a few sentences and Sydney [Rigdon] would write them down, then read them aloud, and if correct, then Joseph would proceed and deliver more."[20] Thus the Lord provided His own preface to His book and called it "my preface unto the book of my commandments" (Doctrine and Covenants 1:6). This revelation was placed at the front of the Book of Commandments and later in the first edition Doctrine and Covenants (1835), where it retained its primacy as section 1.

WITNESSES TO THE BOOK OF COMMANDMENTS (DOCTRINE AND COVENANTS 67)

Following the revelation on the preface to the Book of Commandments, Joseph discussed the principle of witnesses bearing testimony of church scriptural publications, the precedent having been set with the testimonies of the three and eight witnesses to the first edition of the Book of Mormon. The Prophet testified of the blessings associated with being the recipients of modern revelation and "asked the Conference what testimony they were willing to attach to these commandments which should shortly be sent to the world. A number

---

19. W. H. Kelley, "Letter from Elder W. H. Kelley." *The Saints Herald*, (29, 1882, 67).
20. W. H. Kelley, "Letter from Elder W. H. Kelley."

of the brethren arose and said that they were willing to testify to the world that they knew that they were of the Lord."[21]

The Lord then revealed the language of the testimony he wished the brethren to sign as the "Testimony of the Witnesses to the Book of the Lord's Commandments."[22] The plan for publishing the Book of Commandments included placing the Testimony at the conclusion of the book, but the press was destroyed before the printing was complete. After an affirmation of the Testimony by the Twelve Apostles four years later, the Testimony was adapted for publication and included in the first edition of the Doctrine and Covenants published in Kirtland in 1835. In the 21st Century it appears in the "Explanatory Introduction" of the Doctrine and Covenants.

Fears Identified

As noted in the section heading of Doctrine and Covenants 67, "Many of the brethren bore solemn testimony that the revelations then compiled for publication were verily true, as was witnessed by the Holy Ghost shed forth upon them." However, as the conference convened the following day, 2 November, some conference participants expressed a reluctance to affix their names to the Testimony, having not experienced a witness of the Spirit as had the other participants. The Lord responded with another revelation, now known as section 67, a revelation ironically designed to help these brethren receive the revelatory and confirming witness the Lord wished them to have: in one sense a revelation to facilitate the receiving of their own personal revelation. The Lord told the reluctant participants that their "desires have come up before [him]" (verse 1), and that the reason "they did not receive the blessing [the testimony] which offered unto [them]" (verse 3) was that there were "fears in [their] hearts" (verse 3) that stemmed from their judgments that Joseph's "language" contained "imperfections" (verse 5). Some of the brethren were concerned about the Prophet's fitness for being the mouthpiece of the Lord because of

---

21. Minutes, 1–2 November 1831, *The Joseph Smith Papers*, josephsmithpapers. org/paper-summary/minutes-1–2–november-1831/2

22. Testimony, circa 2 November 1831, The Joseph Smith Papers, 29 November 2018, josephsmithpapers.org/paper-summary/testimony-circa-2–november-1831/1

the "misspellings, errors in grammar, and other peculiarities"[23] in the revelations that reflected the limited linguistic skills of an individual whose level of formal education was far below theirs.

This was not the first instance in which Joseph's lack of education had been evident in the process of bringing forth scripture. Emma, Joseph's wife, was intimately aware of the process of translating the Book of Mormon and of her husband's limited abilities, having served as one of his scribes. However, in speaking of the process of translating the Book of Mormon, completed a year and a half earlier from the time of this revelation, Emma did not view Joseph's lack of linguistic skill as a detriment, but rather as evidence that the book was "a marvel and a wonder."[24] Emma later stated in an interview that her husband "could neither write nor dictate a coherent and well-worded letter; let alone dictat[e] a book like the Book of Mormon."[25] She also said that Joseph "had such a limited knowledge of history at that time that he did not even know that Jerusalem was surrounded by walls."[26] Her astonishment and testimony were enhanced as she witnessed the remarkable pattern of her husband resuming translation after interruptions. Joseph would begin where he had left off "without either seeing the manuscript or having any portion of it read to him."[27]

The Lord then challenged the doubting brethren to "seek ye out of the Book of Commandments"(verse 6) one of the revelations they considered to be "the least that is among them," (verse 6) and choose the participant who they considered to be "the most wise" (verse 6) in order to see "if there be any among [them] that shall be able to rewrite the revelation "like unto" (verse 7) the original. If any of them were successful in the attempt, then they would be "justified in saying

23. "I Give Unto You a Testimony of the Truth of These Things," *Doctrine and Covenants Student Manual* (2002), lds.org/manual/doctrine-and-covenants-student-manual/section-67–i-give-you-a-testimony-of-the-truth-of-these-commandments?lang=eng

24. "Last Testimony of Sister Emma," *The Saints' Herald* 26(19) (Oct 1879), 289–90.

25. "Last Testimony of Sister Emma," *The Saints' Herald*.

26. Edmund C. Briggs, "A Visit to Nauvoo in 1856," *Journal of History* vol. 9 no. 4 (Oct. 1916), 454.

27. "Last Testimony of Sister Emma," *The Saints' Herald*.

that [they] did not know that they are true" (verse 7). Otherwise they would be "under condemnation if [they did] not bear record that they are true" (verse 8). He then said that in reality that they had received divine confirmation "there [was][no unrighteousness in them" (verse 9). Some of the participants had apparently forgotten, or disregarded the fact that although he recognized Joseph's limited skills, the Lord himself had just born witness that "these commandments are of me" and labeled them as "mine authority, and the authority of my servants" in his "preface unto the book of my commandments" (Doctrine and Covenants 1:6). He was well aware that his words "were given unto my servants *in their weakness*, after the manner of *their language*, that they might come to understanding (Doctrine and Covenants 1:24, emphasis added).

William McLellin, one of the doubting participants, accepted the Lord's challenge. With an apparent reference to the Lord's words in verse 6, "the most wise among you," the Prophet characterized William as "having more knowledge then sense" in endeavoring to "write a commandment like unto one of the least of the Lord's"— at which William "failed miserably."[28]

Joseph's commentary continued by describing the effect of William's attempt and a reiteration of his role in receiving revelation. "It was an awful responsibility to write in the name of the Lord. The Elders and all present that witnessed this vain attempt of a man to imitate the language of Jesus Christ, renewed their faith in the fulness of the Gospel, and in the truth of the commandments and revelations which the Lord had given to the Church through my instrumentality."[29]

After receiving section 67, five elders likely signed that day, and twelve others signed later.[30] Joseph was apparently less concerned about the exact number of witnesses to these revelations than he had been

---

28. History, 1838–1856, volume A-1 [23 December 805–30 August 1834], 162, The Joseph Smith Papers, josephsmithpapers.org/paper-summary/history-1838–1856–volume-a-1–23–december-1805–30–august-1834/168

29. History, 1838–1856, volume A-1 [23 December 1805–30 August 1834], 162.

30. Testimony, circa 2 November 1831—Historical Introduction, The Joseph Smith Papers, josephsmithpapers.org/paper-summary/testimony-circa-2–november-1831/1

about the three witnesses to the Book of Mormon specified in the Book of Mormon. Anyone who desired to testify was allowed to sign, including individuals not attending the conference. However, Joseph excluded five of the Book of Mormon witnesses in attendance when this revelation was received—Oliver Cowdery and David, John, Christian, and Peter Whitmer, Jr. perhaps, in an effort to increase the number of unique witnesses to the divine origin of the scriptures he had received.

Like many other documents of historical value, the original manuscript of the testimony is not extant, but John Whitmer, the Church historian (see Doctrine and Covenants 47), had copied it into his *Book of Commandment and Revelations*, which was later used as a printer's manuscript. The signatures of the five elders who signed on 2 November appear first on the list; they were copied into the manuscript given to the printer: Sidney Rigdon, Orson Hyde, Wm. E. Mc.lelin [sic], Luke Johnson, and Lyman Johnson. The rest of the signatures of attendees and non-attendees were originals as written in Whitmer's manuscript copy: Reynolds Cahoon probably signed in Hiram, and the rest after John and Oliver took the manuscript to Missouri for printing later in November: Joshua Fairchild, Thomas B. Marsh, Levi Hancock (who added "never to be eraised [sic], John Corrill, Parley Pratt, Harvy Whitlock [sic], Lyman White, Calvin Beebe, and Zebedee Coltrin.[31]

THE LORD'S APPENDIX, DOCTRINE AND COVENANTS 133

Two days after receiving the preface on 1 November, the Lord revealed a concluding section, an appendix, that is now known as section 133. Joseph Smith wrote:

> It had been decided by the conference that Elder Oliver Cowdery should carry the commandments and revelations to Independence, Missouri, for printing, and that I should arrange and get them in readiness by the time that he left, which was to be by—or, if possible, before—the 15th of the month [November]. At this

31. "Remarks of Zebedee Coltrin on Kirtland, Ohio history of the Church," *Minutes, Salt Lake City School of the Prophets, October 3, 1883*, , boap.org/LDS/Early-Saints/ZebC.html

time there were many things which the Elders desired to know relative to preaching the Gospel to the inhabitants of the earth, and concerning the gathering; and in order to walk by the true light, and be instructed from on high, on the 3rd of November, 1831, I inquired of the Lord and received the following important revelation, which has since been added to the book of Doctrine and Covenants, and called the Appendix: [D&C 133]."[32]

The recording of this revelation in *The Book of Commandments and Revelations* does not refer to it as an "appendix," but it may have been understood by the brethren in the conference that it was to serve as such. For example, when Sidney Rigdon made a copy of it he added the label "An appendix to Revelation."[33] When William W. Phelps first published it in the May 1833 issue of *The Evening and the Morning Star*, he explained that it was known as "the close" or "the Appendix,"[34] Unfortunately, the revelation was never published in the Book of Commandments as a result of the 1833 mob violence in Missouri, but Joseph later referred to it as the "appendix" in the 1835 edition of the Doctrine and Covenants because of "its importance, and for distinction."[35]

At the time the first edition of the Doctrine and Covenants was presented to the Church membership in an August 1835 conference for a vote of approval, this appendix appeared as the last section, 100. It was renumbered as section 133 in the 1876 edition.

---

32. History, 1838–1856, volume A-1 [23 December 1805–30 August 1834], 229, *The Joseph Smith Papers*, 10 December 2018, josephsmithpapers.org/paper-summary/history-1838–1856–volume-a-1–23–december-1805–30–august-1834/172.

33. Revelation, 3 November 1831 [D&C 133], "Historical Introduction," The Joseph Smith Papers, 2 December 2018, josephsmithpapers.org/paper-summary/revelation-3–november-1831–dc-133/1#historical-intro.

34. Revelation, 3 November 1831 [D&C 133], "Historical Introduction.

35. History, 1838–1856, volume A-1 [23 December 1805–30 August 1834], 166, The Joseph Smith Papers, 10 December 2018, josephsmithpapers.org/paper-summary/history-1838–1856–volume-a-1–23–december-1805–30–august-1834/172.

CHRONOLOGICAL SUMMARY

1 Nov. 1831:   Four brethren (first of 4 conferences Nov. 11–12; section 68)

1 Nov. 18311:   Preface to the Book of Commandments

2 Nov. 1831:   Challenge to the Prophet's revelatory language (section 67)

2 Nov. 1831:   The Testimony of the Witnesses to the Book of the Lord's Commandments

3 Nov. 1831:   Appendix (second conference; section 133)

8–9 Nov. 1831:   Dealing with revisions (third conference)

Abt. 11 Nov. 1831:   John Whitmer to travel to Missouri (fourth conference; section 69)

11 Nov. 1831:   Church government (section 107; 29 verses)

12 Nov. 1831:   Literacy Firm (section 70)

Chapter 8

"Wherefore, Now Let Every Man Learn His Duty"

Three Revelations Concluding the November Conferences: Doctrine and Covenants 69–70, 107, 103

On 11 and 12 November, the last two days of the series of conference meetings focused on publishing the Book of Commandments, the Lord revealed to the Prophet important practicalities that would move the publication effort forward. He received directions for transporting the printer's manuscript to Missouri, where the Church printer, William W. Phelps, and the Church printing press were located; financial instructions to fund the printing; as well as a revelation on the priesthood.

SECTION 69

On 8 November, the conference appointed Joseph Smith to review the manuscripts and prepare them for publication, correcting "those errors or mistakes which he may discover by the holy Spirit" and having them ready for publication by 15 November, an assignment he completed on time.[1] In July of that year, two other brethren had also been commanded to contribute to this process. Oliver Cowdery, the second elder in the Church (see Doctrine and Covenants 20:2–3; 21:11) had been directed to assist William W. Phelps "in whatsoever place I shall appoint unto him to copy & to correct & select" writings for printing (Doctrine and Covenants 57:13). Following a pattern established with the publication of the Book of Mormon, a copy of the revelations that were to be included in the record book entitled *The Book of Commandments and Revelations* was prepared for transporting to Missouri in order to protect the original hand-written recordings. It became the basis for the printing of the Book of Commandments in 1833 and for the 1835 Doctrine and Covenants.

John Whitmer

On 1 November, the Lord appointed Oliver Cowdery to "carry these sayings" unto the land of Zion" (Doctrine and Covenants 68:33). On the first day of the fourth conference, 11 November, the Lord added, "for my servant Oliver's sake—It is not wisdom in me that he should be entrusted with the commandments and the moneys . . . except one go with who will be true and faithful," (Doctrine and Covenants 69:1), a reference to John Whitmer. The Lord also directed that John "shall continue in writing and making a history" (verse 3), an allusion to a calling John had received two months previously to "serve as the Church historian and recorder, replacing Oliver Cowdery" (Doctrine and Covenants 47, section heading). Before this revelation, the Prophet had invited John to fill this position, to which John replied, "I would rather not do it but observed that the will of the Lord be done, and if he desires it, I desire that he would manifest it through Joseph the Seer" (Doctrine and Covenants 47, section heading). In response to Joseph's petition, the Lord referred to John as "my servant" and directed that John "should write and keep a regular history" (verse 1) and "keep the church record" (verse 3). "After Joseph received this revelation, John accepted and served in his appointed office" (heading, Doctrine and Covenants 47) because he believed he had been "commanded of the

---

1. Minutes, 8 November 1831, *The Joseph Smith Papers*, accessed 21 December 2018, josephsmithpapers.org/paper-summary/minutes-8–november-1831/1.

Lord and Savior Jesus Christ."[2] His formal appointment came a month later on 9 April 1831, when he was assigned "to keep the Church record & history by the voice of ten Elders,"[3] a wise decision in light of the fact that probably "few were as well positioned to observe and record the important events of the church."[4]

John considered his responsibility was to pick up where Oliver Cowdery left off. His records include his intention to "proceed to continue this record,"[5] and then later wrote, "Oliver Cowdery has written the commencement of the church history commencing at the time of the finding of the plates, up to June 12, 1831. From this date I have written the things that I have written."[6]

John had evidenced being "true and faithful" prior to this appointment. He supported the Prophet when he resided with the Whitmer family in Fayette, New York, including serving as a scribe for a portion of the Book of Mormon translation. He was one of the eight witnesses to the Book of Mormon and helped Joseph arrange and copy his revelations in July 1830. A revelation given in June 1829, the first of five revelations directed to him, began with the words "Hearken, my servant John, and listen to the words of Jesus Christ, your Lord and your Redeemer" (Doctrine and Covenants 15:1), and he was later directed to study and preach in the same revelation that the law of common consent was revealed (see Doctrine and Covenants 26) in June 1830. Three months later similar divine direction was given to him in the revelation now known as Doctrine and Covenants 30. The

2. John Whitmer, History, 1831–circa 1847, 1, *The Joseph Smith Papers*, accessed 22 December 2018, josephsmithpapers.org/paper-summary/john-whitmer-history-1831–circa-1847/5#X04FEDC8C-2B6B-4159–A063–6C0B1FA84B78.

3. John Whitmer, History, 1831–circa 1847, "Historical Introduction," *The Joseph Smith Papers*, accessed 22 December 2018, josephsmithpapers.org/paper-summary/john-whitmer-history-1831–circa-1847/5#historical-intro.

4. John Whitmer, History, 1831–circa 1847, "Historical Introduction."

5. John Whitmer, History, 1831–circa 1847, 1, *The Joseph Smith Papers*, accessed 22 December 2018, josephsmithpapers.org/paper-summary/john-whitmer-history-1831–circa-1847/5.

6. John Whitmer, History, 1831–circa 1847, 25, *The Joseph Smith Papers*, accessed 22 December 2018, josephsmithpapers.org/paper-summary/john-whitmer-history-1831–circa-1847/29.

1831 commandments recorded in sections 47 and 69 were the fourth and fifth revelations directed to him. His faithfulness was further demonstrated when he was sent to Kirtland, a month before Joseph arrived, to deal with the problems stemming from a lack of trained priesthood leadership.

Learning to serve as an historian was a lengthy process and required ongoing encouragement from the Prophet and others. As shown, section 69 was the second commandment John had received regarding his responsibility. About a year later, the Prophet wrote in a letter to John: "I exhort Bro John also to remember the commandment to him to keep a history of the church & the gathering and be sure to shew himself approved whereunto he hath been called."[7] In a July 1833 letter, John asked Oliver to request further instructions to which a response was received the following January.[8] In John's patriarchal blessing, given by the Prophet himself in September 1835, concern was expressed for the history he was writing, and he was promised that he "shall make a choice record of Israel."[9] (John's subsequent history appears in the notes.)

SECTION 107

November 11 also saw the reception of a revelation dealing with organizational structures in Church administration and the responsibilities associated with quorum leadership. The exact context for the revelation is unknown, but historical records do indicate that Reynolds Cahoon's question of whether he should travel to Missouri the following spring was discussed in a conference of elders held on that day. Besides discussing Reynolds' question, Oliver Cowdery read "Commandments concerning the duties of the Elders"[10] during which this revelation may have also been received. It now appears as verses 58–100 of section 107 and includes inspired changes that were made

7. John Whitmer, History, 1831–circa 1847, "Historical Introduction."
8. Ibid.
9. Ibid.
10. Minutes, 11 Nov. 1831. *The Joseph Smith Papers*, accessed 24 November 2020, josephsmithpapers.org/paper-summary/minutes-11–november-1831/1.

to some of the verses while the Prophet was preparing the revelations for publication in the 1835 Doctrine and Covenants.

This 1831 revelation contains an allusion to the "church laws respecting church business" (verse 59). These laws probably include the three revelations known as the "Articles and Covenants," most of which was given around 6 April 1830 in the Peter Sr. and Mary Whitmer home in Fayette, New York (Doctrine and Covenants 20), the "Laws of the Church of Christ" given on 9 and 23 February in the Newell K. and Elizabeth Ann Whitney home in Kirtland (Doctrine and Covenants 42), and a portion of a revelation given 1 November 1831 in the Johnsons' home (Doctrine and Covenants 68:13–24) ten days prior to the reception of this portion of section 107.

This portion comprises about half of the latter verses of section 107, and the circumstances surrounding the reception of the first half are indicative of the revelatory process surrounding the Prophet's preparation of the revelations for the first edition of the Doctrine and Covenants. In March 1835, a month after the Quorum of the Twelve Apostles was first organized, the First Presidency and the Twelve decided the Twelve should travel to the eastern branches and conduct a series of local conferences. These conferences were to be held "for the purpose of regulateing all things necessary"[11] in response to "the many pressing requests from the eastern churches."[12] To prepare the Twelve for this mission, Joseph presented to them a compilation of revelations that was later entitled "On Priesthood" (section 3) in the 1835 edition of the Doctrine and Covenants and is currently numbered as section 107. It comprises one of the premier sections outlining doctrines of the priesthood and the structures of priesthood organizations and represents the inspired interweaving of two 1835 revelatory recordings, inspired insights contributed by the Prophet, the 1831 revelation, and two unpublished revelations. One such revelation detailing bishop

---

11. Record of the Twelve, 14 February–28 August 1835, 4, *The Joseph Smith Papers*, accessed 30 December 2018, josephsmithpapers.org/paper-summary/record-of-the-twelve-14–february-28–august-1835/10.

12. Instruction on Priesthood, between circa 1 March and circa 4 May 1835 [Doctrine and Covenants 107], *The Joseph Smith Papers*, accessed 30 December 2018, josephsmithpapers.org/paper-summary/instruction-on-priesthood-between-circa-1–march-and-circa-4–may-1835–dc-107/1#historical-intro;).

responsibilities was revealed in mid-March 1832 in the Johnsons' home, and the other was probably received in January 1833 calling Frederick G. Williams to replace Jesse Gause as a counselor to the Prophet.[13] (See chapter 12, which includes the contributions of section 107 for a treatment of the evolution of the First Presidency.) This compilation of revelations provides doctrinal insights about the priesthood beyond what had already been revealed and important clarifications and elaborations on the government of the Church, including explanations of the duties of Church officers. (Verses 53–55 regarding Adam-ondi-Ahman are of special interest.)[14]

SECTION 70

On the last day of the conferences, 12 November, the Prophet expressed the desire that Oliver Cowdery, John Whitmer, and "the sacred writings which they have entrusted to them to carry to Zion be

---

13. Revelation, 5 January 1833, The Joseph Smith Papers, accessed 31 December 2018, josephsmithpapers.org/paper-summary/revelation-5–january-1833/1.

14. Verse 53–55 describe a meeting of Adam with his righteous posterity in the valley of Adam-ondi-ahman. It has been thought that these verses were revealed on December 18, 1833 while Joseph ordained his father as the first Church patriarch in the Johnson Inn in Kirtland (Joseph Fielding Smith, ed., Teachings of the Prophet Joseph Smith, (Salt Lake City, UT: Deseret Book, 1976, 38). However, although Joseph Smith, Sr. did receive a blessing of some sort that day along with several others, he was not ordained a patriarch until a year later, December 6, 1834, when he was also ordained "Assistant President of the Church of the Latter-day Saints" (Blessing from Joseph Smith Sr., 9 December 1834, The Joseph Smith Papers, accessed 1 January 2019, josephsmithpapers.org/paper-summary/blessing-from-joseph-smith-sr-9–december-1834/1#historical-intro). It is now known these words were part of the 1835 section "On Priesthood." Interestingly, in September 1835, when Oliver Cowdery recorded the 1833 blessings in his patriarchal blessing book, he added these "words . . . fell from his (Joseph's) lips while the visions of the Almighty were open to his view" when recording it (Appendix 5: Blessings, September and October 1835, Introduction, The Joseph Smith Papers, accessed 2 January 2019, josephsmithpapers.org/paper-summary/appendix-5–blessings-september-and-october-1835–introduction/1)   thus adding to the list of appearances of deity to the Prophet that occurred in Kirtland.

dedicated to the Lord by the prayer of faith."[15] He further moved that he and his former and current scribes be recompensed for their service. "Secondly, Br. Oliver has labored with me from the begining in writing &c. Br. Martin [Harris] has labored with me from the begining, & brs. John & Sidney also for a considerable time,4 & as these sacred writings are now going to the Church for their benefit, that we may have claim on the Church for recompence."[16] Additionally, the conference voted to prize "the book of Revelation now to be printed being the foundation of the Church & the salvation of the world & the Keys of the mysteries of the Kingdom & the riches of Eternity to the Church."[17]

The last of the eight revelations associated with the publication, now numbered as section 70, may have been given in response to the Prophet's desires expressed in the conference and was either revealed during the conference or shortly after it was adjourned. The above-named brethren were "appointed" and "ordained . . . to be stewards over the revelations and commandments" (verse 3), and the Lord labeled this stewardship as "their business in the Church of God" (verse 5), thus establishing the roots of what came to be known as the Literary Firm.

This stewardship was founded on principles associated with the law of consecration that were revealed elsewhere. In section 70, the Lord said "an account of this stewardship will I require" just as He "requires of every man in his stewardship" so that in "temporal things [they should] be equal" (verses 3–4, 9). It was responsible for the printing and distribution of Church publications while providing resources "for food and for rainment, for an inheritance; for houses and for lands" for full-time Church leadership. Proceeds that enabled the brethren to "receive more than is needful" were to "given unto my storehouse" (verse 7) as well "consecrated unto the inhabitants of Zion" (verse 8).

---

15. Minutes, 12 November 1831, The Joseph Smith Papers, accessed 23 December 2018, josephsmithpapers.org/paper-summary/minutes-12–november-1831/1).

16. Ibid.

17. Ibid.

PUBLICATION DIFFICULTIES IN MISSOURI

Oliver Cowdery and John Whitmer left Hiram, Ohio, on 20 November with the revelation book in hand and arrived in Independence, Missouri, on 5 January 1832. The plan was to print Joseph Smith's revelations, The Book of Commandments, along with the Bible translation, a Church almanac, children's literature, and Church newspapers including *The Evening and the Morning Star*. In April 1832, the Prophet and other members of the Firm traveled to Independence to finalize the plans for publishing 10,000 copies of the revelations, a number later reduced to 3,000. Early the following year, the first twenty-five revelations were published in *The Evening and the Morning Star*, the Church newspaper in Missouri, then reset for printing in the Book of Commandments. The Prophet approved the page proofs when they were sent to Kirtland, but unfortunately, the publication of the Book of Commandments was never completed.

The Missouri Saints were violently persecuted in 1833 over their differences with the original Jackson County settlers regarding economics, politics, culture, and religion. The violence escalated when the pro-slavery settlers were angered by the publication of an editorial, "Free People of Color," which lead to the fear that the Latter-day Saints, who numbered nearly 1,200, were encouraging the immigration of free African Americans to the county. Ironically, the editorial had been designed to calm those fears. On July 20, 1833, the printing press in Independence was destroyed by a mob who also threw the first five printing signatures—thirty-two were needed—into a bonfire outside the printing office. The printing office, which included the second-story home of the Phelps family, was leveled and their furniture destroyed.

In an extraordinary act of courage, Mary Elizabeth Rollins and her younger sister Caroline collected a large number of the printed signatures. When the mob ordered them to stop, the girls fled to a nearby cornfield where they laid on top of the signatures, silently praying for protection. They heard members of the mob treading the corn near their position, but the men were unable to find them. Meanwhile a young man, John Taylor (not the future President of the Church), risked his life in a similar courageous act. He saw that some of the signatures had been dumped in a log stable, so he quietly approached the stable without being seen, reached through the logs, and pulled out multiple sheets at a time. He was seen by the mob who threw stones at him, but he escaped with a helpful collection of signatures. As a result, in large measure due to these courageous acts, about one hundred, 160-page printings were eventually published. These represented 58 of the first 64 sections of the eventual first edition Doctrine and Covenants, along with 47 verses of a chapter we now know as section 64.

MULTIPLE EDITIONS: THE PRINTING CONTINUES

Undaunted, the Firm moved to Kirtland and expanded its publication efforts by printing newspapers—the *Messenger and Advocate* and the *Northern Times*, which were reprints of *The Evening and the Morning Star* and the *Elders' Journal*, a second edition Book of Mormon, the first edition of the Doctrine and Covenants, and a hymnal. Other firms were established (see (Doctrine and Covenants 78) and combined with the Literary Firm to create the United Firm, which served as a business management organization. In 1834, members of the United Firm voted to dissolve it. Thirteen days later, the Lord revealed that the firms were to be reorganized and individuals, including John Johnson, be given stewardship of a number of "businesses." Oliver Cowdery and Frederick G Williams were assigned the publishing stewardship (see Doctrine and Covenants 104:29–32; 58–59) and eventually Oliver became the sole editor and publisher when he bought out Frederick. While the whole Church was reeling from the collapse of the Kirtland Safety Society in 1837, the printing office in Kirtland next to the Temple closed its doors over issues relating to finances and management before most the Saints began their exodus to Missouri. It was destroyed by fire shortly thereafter.

CHRONOLOGICAL SUMMARY

Oct. 1831:   Revelations for William McLellin about the kingdom of God (sections 65 and 66)

Nov. 1831:   Several conferences—publishing revelations

Dec. 1831:   JST interrupted for dealing with apostates, anti-Latter-day Saints (section 71)

Dec. 1831:   Joseph to Kirtland, revelation on bishop's storehouses, second bishop (section 72)

Jan. 1832:   Bible translation resumes (section 73)

25 Jan. 1832:   Joseph sustained as President of the High Priesthood (section 75)

Chapter 9

"Confound Your Enemies"

Doctrine and Covenants 71, 73, 126

DELAY THE BIBLE TRANSLATION

Following the ending of the series of four conferences focused on publishing the Book of Commandments on November 12, 1831, the Prophet and Sidney Rigdon resumed their Bible translation. Just two and a half weeks later, they were directed in section 71 to temporarily stop translating in order to deal with the anti-Latter-day Saint sentiment being instigated by former Church members in the Hiram area. They joined other missionaries already serving in aggressively declaring and defending the message of the Restoration by "call(ing) upon (your enemies) to meet you both in public and in private" (verse 6).

Persecution of the Saints began long before the Church was formally organized and continued when the Church moved to Ohio. Many former Ohio members were very active in fomenting this opposition, including two leading figures in the Hiram area, Symonds Ryder and Ezra Booth, typical of many who leave the Church. Interestingly, the brighter parts of Symond's and Ezra's brief church membership began with the Johnsons, but their commitment was short-lived.

SYMONDS RYDER

Symonds Ryder was one of Hiram's earliest Latter-day Saint converts as well as one of its earliest settlers. Born in Vermont in 1792, Symonds came to Hiram, Ohio, in 1814 and settled on land just east of the eventual Johnson property, resulting in the Ryders and the Johnsons becoming well-connected. Besides being neighbors, Symonds' wife, Mehetable Loomis, had traveled from Vermont with the Johnsons and was probably a relative.[1] The Ryders and Johnsons were also connected because Symonds' younger brother, Jason, married Fanny Johnson, one of John and Elsa's older children. Symonds even lent the Johnsons money and witnessed all of their property transactions before 1832. This connection no doubt led to Symonds' later characterizing John Johnson as "one of our most worthy men.[2]

Symonds described the religious environment of Hiram around the time of the coming of the missionaries. "It has been stated that from the year 1815 to 1835, a period of twenty years, all sorts of doctrines, by all sorts of preachers, have been plead; and most of the people of Hiram had been disposed to turn out and hear."[3] He and his family had joined the Campbellite (later called the Disciples of Christ) movement in 1828 in nearby Mantua and then participated in the branch in Hiram with Sidney Rigdon as their itinerant leader. His conversion to the Church appears to have stemmed from witnessing the healing of Elsa Johnson's arm (see chapter 2) and hearing a young girl prophesy of an earthquake in China that was later fulfilled. As a later Disciples of Christ leader B. A. Hinsdale put it, "Ryder had never been satisfied that the Disciples did justice to the Scripture doctrine of spiritual gifts; and it was the pretended miracles of Smith, some of which were very extraordinary, that led him to embrace the new faith."[4]

---

1. Mark L. Staker, *Hearken, O Ye People* (Salt Lake City: Greg Kofford Books, 2009, 357–362.
2. Symonds Ryder, "Letter to A. S. Hayden," in Amos Sutton Hayden, *Early History of the Disciples in the Western* Reserve (Chase and Hall: Cincinnati, OH, 1876), 221.
3. Ibid., 220.
4. Symonds Ryder, "letter of Symonds Ryder," in B. A. Hinsdale, *A History of*

He and Mehetable were baptized in June 1831, two of many Campbellites. Depicting the Latter-day Saint influence in the area, Hinsdale mockingly recorded, "How many Disciples were seduced from the faith and were joined to the new idols, probably cannot now be determined; but so many were, that for the time it seemed as though the Church would be broken up. . . . The defection of Symonds Ryder was felt to be a severe blow."[5]

Symonds was ordained an elder the same month of his baptism and was also in attendance at the June conference on the Morley farm. There he was called to take the place of Heman Basset in accompanying several brethren who were assigned to travel to Missouri (see Doctrine and Covenants 52:37).

Symonds' refusal to accept this calling shortly after his baptism accompanied a disillusionment with the Church, although here is some evidence that Symonds' wife, Mehetable, did not agree with him and had a stronger commitment to follow the counsel of Joseph Smith for a time. Having observed the sacrifice of property by Isaac and Lucy Morley in responding to the call to move to Missouri, he became uncomfortable with the apparent control over members' property the law of consecration and stewardship provided the Prophet. Although somewhat exaggerative, Symonds suggested that he was not the only Hiram area convert concerned about sacrificing property. "This was too much for the Hiramites, and they left the Mormonites faster than they ever joined them, and by fall, the Mormon Church in Hiram was a very lean concern."[6] A second possible reason for Symonds' disillusionment can be attributed to Hinsdale, who stated Symonds left the Church as a result of a misspelling of his name in section 52—"Was the Holy Spirit so fallible as to fail even in orthography?"[7]—although the standardized spelling of names and other words was not yet a common characteristic of American English in this period. (This claim has led to

---

the Disciples in Hiram, Portage Co., O. (Cleveland, OH: Robison, Savage, and Company), 19.

5. Symonds Ryder, "letter of Symonds Ryder," 19.
6. B. A. Hinsdale, *A History of the Disciples in Hiram, Portage Co., O.* (Cleveland, OH: Robison, Savage, and Company, 1876), 19.
7. Ibid., 252.

the long-time vilification of Symonds based on the misspelling that appears in numerous Church publications, but Hinsdale is the only source for it.) By September 1831, he had left the Church and publicly announced his opposition in a letter entitled "Secret Bye Laws of the Mormonites" that was published in two local newspapers.[8] In it he quoted all of section 42, a portion of which was published, and used his misinterpretation of the law of consecration to portray it as an attempt to defraud the Saints. (Symonds' handwritten copy includes the most complete extant copy of section 42 and is the one published in the *Joseph Smith Papers.*[9]) He may have been one of the leaders of the mob that tarred and feathered Joseph and Sidney in March 1832,[10] although Ryder family records would indicate otherwise. After leaving the Church, Symonds resumed his Campbellite affiliation in Hiram, serving as an elder. Of his relationship with the Disciples Hinsdale wrote:

> He soon won back the confidence of his brethren and was held in as high esteem as ever. This Mormon episode in the history of Hiram is most remarkable. It was nothing less than a temporary madness. Those who gave way to it were not adjudged fickle or unstable by their neighbors. "You were a Mormon" never became an expression of reproach.[11]

As a religious leader and prosperous farmer, Symonds had been highly esteemed and his temporary conversion did not seem to result in any permanent damage to his reputation among former and non-latter-day Saints. He later became one of the founders of Hiram College.

---

8. "Secret Bye Laws of the Mormonites," Western Courier (Ravenna, OH), 1 Sept. 1831; "Secret Bye Laws of the Mormonites," Painesville (OH) Telegraph, 13 Sept. 1831.
9. Revelation, 9 February 1831 [Doctrine and Covenants 42:1–72], The Joseph Smith Papers, 23 May 2019, josephsmithpapers.org/paper-summary/revelation-9–february-1831–dc-421–72/1#7866403746311282104.
10. History, 1838–1856, volume A-1 [23 December 1805–30 August 1834]," p. 206, The Joseph Smith Papers, October 29, 2018, josephsmithpapers.org/paper-summary/history-1838–1856–volume-a-1–23–december-1805–30–august-1834/212.
11. B. A. Hinsdale, *A History of the Disciples in Hiram, Portage Co., O*, 20.

EZRA BOOTH

Ezra Booth was a former Methodist circuit preacher who had settled in Nelson, near Hiram, to take up farming but was induced to
return to preaching by the local population. He was a "man of considerable culture and eloquence,"[12] as shown in this somewhat humorous
statement by Ezra regarding the Native Americans in the area.

> It is pleasing to see the sturdy towering trees of the forest falling
> prostrate before the industrious husbandman but it is infinitely
> more pleasing to behold the prostrate worshipers of Jehovah who
> have assembled from the different parts of the wilderness to pay
> divine homage to their God, and where the howlings of the beast
> of prey and the horrid yell of the uncivilized savage was to be heard
> a few years since is now made vocal with the transporting sound of
> the Gospel and the melodious songs of Zion.[13]

The Johnsons were among Ezra's earliest Methodist converts in
the area when they joined his congregation in 1826.

As stated in chapter 2, Ezra subsequently joined the Church
after studying the Book of Mormon with the Johnsons and witnessing the miracle healing of Elsa Johnson's arm. Even after he
had eventually apostatized, Ezra Booth later reflected: "When I
embraced Mormonism, I conscientiously believed it to be of God.
The impressions of my mind were deep and powerful, and my
feelings were excited to a degree to which I had been a stranger.
Like a ghost, it haunted me by night and by day. . . . At times I
was much elated."[14]

Ezra immediately began preaching the doctrines of the Restoration
and due to his already widespread reputation was influential in win-
ning a number of converts. He participated in the June 1831 conference in Kirtland, and there was ordained a high priest and called to

---

12. Eliott I. Osgood, *Centennial History of the Hiram Church 1835–1935* (1935), 5.
13. Ezra Booth, "To the Editors of the Methodist Magazine," [no month] 1819,
    1, cited in Richard S. Van Wagoner, *Polygamy: A* History (Salt Lake City:
    Signature Books, 1989), 277; 13 May 2019, sidneyrigdon.com/features/
    hiram2.htm.
14. Ezra Booth to Ira Eddy, Sept. 1831, in E. D. Howe, *Mormonism Unvailed* [sic]
    (1834), 176.

accompany Isaac Morley as one of several missionaries to Missouri (see Doctrine and Covenants 52:23).

Ezra hesitated briefly but then departed on 15 June. His missionary experience was not nearly as rewarding as his previous preaching of the Restoration in the Hiram area nor his prior Methodist service. He was not very successful, did not experience the spiritual manifestations such as miracles and the gift of tongues which he expected would have furthered his commitment to the Church, was disappointed by the barrenness of western Missouri, and was surprised by the small numbers of Church members there. His irritation was exacerbated by two elements related to his return to Hiram. First, he and Isaac initially joined Joseph and the other missionaries as they traveled by canoe. As the river waters became dangerous, causing one canoe to capsize and nearly capsizing others, tempers flared and Joseph was criticized by many of the missionaries, including Ezra. He later wrote reflectingly: "These are the men whom the Lord has intrused the mysteries, and the keys of the kingdom. . . . These are the leaders of the Church, and the only Church on earth the Lord beholds with approbation."[15]

Second, Ezra and his companion, Isaac Morley, ignored the divine direction to "preach the word by the way" (Doctrine and Covenants 52:23), which meant walking most of the way back. He had observed that Joseph and Sidney were allowed to travel portions of the journey to and from Missouri in more comfortable conveyances, while a man of his stature and prestige was consigned to walking a substantial part of the 1800–mile round trip. His attitude led Isaac and him to continue on canoes, then travel by steamboat and stagecoach rather than walk back to Ohio.

Ezra returned to Hiram on 1 September, and on 6 September was "silenced from preaching as an Elder in this Church"[16] by a conference in Nelson. He did not react well five days later when the Lord revealed that He "was angry with him who was my servant Ezra Booth, and also my servant Isaac Morley, for they kept not the law, neither the commandment" (Doctrine and Covenants 64:15) and that "there are

---

15. "Mormonism—No. VII," *Ohio Star*, Nov. 21, 1831.
16. Minutes, 6 September 1831, The Joseph Smith Papers, 24 May 2019, josephsmithpapers.org/paper-summary/minutes-6–september-1831/1.

those who have sought occasion again him (Joseph) without cause" (Doctrine and Covenants 64:6). Digging deeper, the Prophet said Ezra struggled "when he actually learned that faith, humility, patience, and tribulation go before blessing, and that . . . he must become all things to all men, that he might peradventure save some."[17] Fortunately, Isaac humbled himself and went on to a lifetime of church service and leadership in Missouri, Nauvoo, and Utah. Ezra's excommunication soon followed, and he, along with Symonds Ryder, publicly renounced the Restoration at a Methodist camp meeting at nearby Shalersville. He even went so far as to write Edward Partridge in Missouri, attempting him to leave the Church, a letter Edward ignored.

In order to return to the good graces of Methodist leadership, Ezra accepted their invitation to attempt to undo the "damage" his Restoration preaching had caused by writing a series of nine letters outlining his complaints against the church in the local newspaper printed in Ravenna, the *Ohio Star*. These complaints included the authoritarian Church hierarchy, the behavior of Church leaders that he deemed inconsistent with the revelations, false prophecies and the hiding of revelations from the public, contention among Church members, and the Prophet's jovial nature which Ezra did not consider consistent with the Prophet's calling—"a want of . . . sobriety, prudence, and stability, . . . a spirit of lightness and levity, a temper of mind easily irritated, and an habitual proneness to jesting and joking."[18]

SECTIONS 71 AND 73

The defection of Symonds and Ezra, along with other former members, began to seriously affect the work of the Church in the Hiram area. In response, the Lord revealed on 1 December 1831 that Joseph and Sidney should "open (their) mouths in proclaiming my gospel, . . . confound[ing] . . . your enemies in public and in private" in the Hiram area "for the space of a season, even until it shall be made known unto you" (Doctrine and Covenants 71:1–2, 3, 7). Joseph

---

17. *History of the Church* 1:16.
18. "Mormonism—No. VII," *Ohio Star*, Nov. 21, 1831.

and Sidney immediately complied by laying aside the translation and began preaching throughout the area for the next five weeks. Their efforts included challenging Ezra and Symonds to a public debate scheduled for Christmas Day in the Ravenna schoolhouse. While Symonds declined, Ezra accepted the challenge but failed to appear. Sidney took this opportunity and preached for two successive days with great success.

By 10 January 1832, "much was accomplished in diminishing the unfavorable feelings that had arisen against the Church" (Doctrine and Covenants 73 heading), and Joseph reported that their work "did much towards allaying the excited feelings which were growing out of the scandalous letters then being published."[19] As a result, Joseph and Sidney were told that it was "expedient to translate again" (Doctrine & Covenants 73:3). Unfortunately, Ezra's letters were circulated extensively and later were used as an important source for the first anti-Latter-day Saint book, Eber D. Howe's highly damaging *Mormonism Unvailed*, published in 1834.

As indicated, Symonds returned to local Campbellite leadership and Ezra to his Methodist preaching. In fulfillment of the Prophet's apparent prophecy, "if you turn against us, you will enjoy no more satisfaction in the world,"[20] Ezra's commitment to Methodism was short-lived. After just a few years, he followed after William Miller's Second Adventism, which proclaimed the Second Coming of Christ would occur in 1844. When the time passed, "he ceased to pray, abandoned Christianity and became an agnostic."[21]

TAR AND FEATHERING

Although the work in response to section 71 had a positive effect, the stage was set for continuing animosity and unrest by at least three factors. First, as suggested by Symonds Ryder's reaction, one of the most unsettling Latter-day Saint teachings was the call for many of

---

19. *History of the Church* 1:241.
20. Mormonism—No. VII," *Ohio Star*, Nov. 21, 1831.
21. J. N. Fradenburgh, *History of Erie Conference* (Oil City, PA: Derrick Publishing Compay, 1907, 346).

the Saints to gather to Missouri. Of the hundreds of converts made in the Hiram area, over one hundred planned to gather, affecting families and the economy of most neighborhoods. Important businesses, including a blacksmith, a stone mason, and a carding mill would close, and extended families would be separated. As in the case of Mehetable and Symonds Ryder, as well as the local teacher, Benjamin Hinckley, and his wife, Susanna, some married couples were divided as to the issue of gathering. Second, both family and economic effects also stemmed from concerns about the law of consecration. Those gathering to Missouri were commanded to consecrate all their possessions, receiving an inheritance in return. Family members who remained behind feared the threat to their livelihoods if they partnered with Missouri gatherers.[22] Third, doctrinal differences contributed to the contention and Sidney connected the tar and feathering at Hiram to the vision of the three degrees of glory.[23]

Those gathering to Missouri met at the Johnsons' home in preparation for their move in March 1832. Many residents who were opposed to the move attended the meeting to angrily express their concerns and threaten Joseph and Sidney. In his rebuke, the Prophet apparently guaranteed the Lord would protect him and his counselors.[24] In reply, the opposition promised that Joseph and Sidney would be mobbed. In March, someone bored a hole in the cabin where the Rigdons were staying which was across Pioneer Trail from the Johnsons' home and filled it with gun powder. Their noise attracted the attention of some guests of the Rigdons causing the would-be arsonist to run off. This opposition "ripened to open war"[25] and climaxed with one of the most heinous acts of persecution ever heaped upon the Prophet—the tar and feathering, a typical practice of vigilante justice in early America.

On the cold night of Saturday, 24 March, a mob of men numbering about thirty and consisting of mostly apostates who had relatives that

---

22. Symonds Ryder, "Letter to A. S. Hayden," 221.
23. Thomas Bullock, Minutes of April Conference, Nauvoo, Illinois, April 6, 1844.
24. Hartwell Ryder, "A Short History of the Foundation of the Mormon Church," (1902), 4; Geauga Gazette, 17 April 1832).
25. History of Portage County, Ohio, 16b, 24 May 2019, sidneyrigdon.com/RigdonO3.htm#1874–016a.

were faithful latter-day Saints, gathered at the brickyard of Benjamin Hinckley, an apostate whose wife Susannah was and remained faithful, about a mile east of the Johnsons' home. After laying specific plans, the mobbers blackened their faces, drank some "liquid courage" (alcohol) and split into two groups of approximately the same number. One group stealthily marched to the residence of the Prophet and his family in the Johnsons' home while the other group went to the residence of Sydney Rigdon and his family.

Sidney and his family were asleep on the second floor of the cabin when the mob broke through the door. They climbed the stairs and dragged Sidney out of bed and down the stairs. The trauma associated with his head bouncing on the frozen ground and possibly the staircase, along with the beating he received, knocked him unconscious and severely injured his head and body. He was beaten and tarred and feathered while in this state and then left alone. When his wife, Phebe, went looking for him she found he had regained some consciousness but was delirious and disoriented. She escorted him back to their cabin and did what she could to ease his suffering. It took several days for him to regain a measure of health, and his damaged mental capacity was not immediately alleviated.

Joseph had this to say about Sidney's condition.

> The next morning I went to see Elder Rigdon and found him crazy, and his head highly inflamed, for they had dragged him by his heels, and those, too, so high from the ground that he could not raise his head from the rough, frozen surface, which lacerated it exceedingly; and when he saw me he called to his wife to bring him his razor. She asked him what he wanted of it; and he replied, to kill me. Sister Rigdon left the room, and he asked me to bring his razor. I asked him what he wanted of it, and he replied he wanted to kill his wife; and he continued delirious some days. The feathers which were used with the tar on this occasion, the mob took out of Elder Rigdon's house. After they had seized him, and dragged him out, one of the banditti returned to get some pillows; when the women shut him in and kept him a prisoner some time.[26]

26. *History of the Church* 1:265.

By Wednesday he was well enough to move his family and planned to settle them in Kirtland, but fearing mob violence moved his family to Chardon instead. He then joined Joseph, Jesse Gause, the other counselor to Joseph, Peter Whitmer Jr., and Newell K. Whitney in Warren, Ohio, in early April and accompanied them to Missouri.

Sidney never fully recovered. He suffered mental and emotional effects for the rest of his life that varied in severity and timing. Newell K. Whitney recorded that following the event, Sidney was "either in the bottom of the cellar or up in the garrett window."[27]

There were times he was quite coherent and in possession of all his mental capacities, which enabled him to continue to offer great service in the cause of the Restoration. For example, four years after the trauma he managed to deliver a sermon at the Kirtland Temple dedication that held nearly one thousand congregants spellbound for two and one-half hours. On the other hand, the brain injury may have been the root cause of his "Salt Sermon" that incited Missouri mobs in 1838, the mental state that precipitated his early release from Liberty Jail, his inability to leave his bed for several days at a time while living in Nauvoo, the Prophet's desire to release him from the First Presidency in Nauvoo, and his offering himself as a "Guardian for the Church" at the time of the Prophet's martyrdom. It was not surprising, therefore, that he was excommunicated, but a knowledge of his damaged mental condition provides a more merciful lens when judging Sidney's actions later in his life. He returned to Pennsylvania, the state of his upbringing, following his excommunication. He associated with the James J. Strang movement which sought to install Strang as the president of the Church. Following disassociating with Strang, he started his own splinter group, which William Bickerton subsequently led following Sidney's exit and is still functioning today as the Church of Jesus Christ, or "Bickertonites" with approximately 20,000 members.[28] However, despite all of this struggle, his son

27. Bruce Van Orden, "Rigdon, Sidney," Daniel H. Ludlow, ed., *Encyclopedia of Mormonism* (New York: MacMillan Publishing Company, 1992, 1234).

28. List of Denominations in the Latter-day Saint Movement, 25 May 2019, worddisk.com/wiki/List_of_sects_in_the_Latter_Day_Saint_movement/.

records Sidney's unflinching testimony of the mission of the Prophet and the Restoration.

While these horrific things were being done to Sidney, the other part of the mob focused their designs on the Prophet. The stage had been set by John Johnson's apostate brother, Eli, who either working alone or with another mobber, Miles Norton,[29] killed the dog to avoid it sounding an alarm, rendered the Johnsons' guns useless by inserting dirt or other objects into them, and by leaving the door to the home unlocked. Joseph and Emma, who was about seven weeks pregnant, were up part of the night tending to their adopted ten–month-old twins, Julia and Joseph, who were sick with the measles. (There is some question among historians regarding the location of the bedroom Joseph and Emma used, as well as the exact location where Joseph was taken. References in this regard are available in the footnotes of this chapter.[30] The exact locations are not nearly as important to the story as the actual events that testify of the incredible courage and commitment of the Smiths, Rigdons, and Johnsons.) When young Joseph fell asleep Emma suggested her husband lay down with him on the trundle bed while she would remained with Julia on the main bed. After Julia fell asleep, Emma dozed off as well but was soon awakened by the sound of scratching on a window, of which Joseph said Emma "took no particular notice of but which was unquestionably design'd for ascertaining whether we were all asleep."[31] Then the door to the outside burst open, and in rushed approximately twelve members of the mob. Amidst Emma's screams, several of them grabbed Joseph by the legs, arms, and hair. He struggled so strenuously that the one holding his hair, Carnot Mason, an apostate member, yanked out a large swath, leaving a bald spot. While

---

29. E. Cecil McGavin, *The Historical Background of the* Doctrine and Covenants (Salt Lake City: Paragon Printing Company, 1949) as found in Mark L. Staker, *Hearken, O Ye People* (Salt Lake City: Greg Kofford Books, 2009, 364).

30. Mark L. Staker, *Hearken, O Ye People* (Salt Lake City: Greg Kofford Books, 2009, 357–362); Karl R. Anderson, Personal Communication, November 39, 2018.

31. *History of the Church* 1:261

being carried out the door, Joseph managed to free one leg and kicked Warren Waste, a man known in the region for his strength and wrestling ability, and "sent him sprawling in the street."[32] Warren is quoted as saying, "Do not let him touch the ground, or he will run over the whole of us."[33] Joseph recounted: "I was immediately confined again; and they swore by God, they would kill me if I did not be still, which quieted me. As they passed around the house with me, the fellow that I kicked came to me and thrust his hand into my face, (for I hit him on the nose,) and with an exulting horse laugh, muttered, _____ _____ ye; I'll fix ye. They then seized me by the throat, and held on till I lost my breath."[34]

Joseph fell unconscious and then awakened shortly thereafter while being carried past the body of Sidney Rigdon. Assuming he was dead, Joseph pleaded for his life, "You will have mercy and spare my life, I hope."[35] His requst was met with cursing and derision.

When they arrived at the designated place of seclusion for the tar and feathering, Joseph's clothes were ripped off of him and one mobber scratched him all over his body remarking, "That's the way the Holy Ghost falls on folks."[36] Joseph was severely kicked and beaten. Then a bucket of "tar," which was probably unheated pine sap, was spread over his body. An attempt was made to also jam the wooden paddle used to spread the tar into his mouth, but Joseph's writhing prevented it. A doctor among the mob, Richard Dennison, brought along glass vials of "aqua fortis," a medical concoction when used in small amounts currently known as nitric acid. Joseph's clenched teeth prevented the doctor from being able to pour a glass vial into Joseph's mouth, so he pounded on Joseph's teeth with the vial, attempting to cause Joseph to open his mouth. Instead, a tooth was chipped and the vial broke, splashing the

---

32. Luke Johnson, "History of Luke Johnson," *Millennial Star* 26(53) (December 31, 1864), 834.
33. George A. Smith, *Journal of Discourses,* November 15, 1864, 11:6.
34. *History of the Church* l:261–262.
35. *History of the Church* 1:262
36. *History of the Church* 1:263.

burning concoction on his cheeks. About that time, approaching noises were heard and the mobbers scattered.

The Prophet's ability to endure this torturous treatment may have been enhanced by an out-of-body experience. Heber C. Kimball stated: "Joseph's life was at stake then he had been mobbed and slain I heard him say himself when they killed his body and his spirit was in the heavens looking down upon his body and saw the mob pouring aqua fortis down his neck trying to break his neck and calling upon him to call upon his God to help him."[37]

When Joseph gained consciousness, he had to pull tar away from his mouth in order to breathe and then walked as guided by a small, distant light emanating from the Johnsons' home. "When I came to the door I was naked, and the tar made me look as if I were covered with blood, and when my wife saw me she thought I was all crushed to pieces, and fainted."[38] Members that had gathered at the Johnsons' home covered him with a blanket and took him into the house. They had to scrape his skin in order to remove the tar and then otherwise tended to his wounds, which probably included broken ribs.[39] The next morning was Sunday and Joseph reported, "With my flesh all scarfied and defaced, I preached to the congregation as usual," either from the front porch of the Johnsons' home if the weather permitted, or in the school house owned by Benjamin Hinckley that was used for meetings in inclement weather. The topic of the sermon is unknown, but some of the mob members, as well as Symonds Ryder, who was accompanied by his wife, Mehetable, were in the congregation, apparently attempting to disguise their involvement with the mob. Despite

---

37. Heber C. Kimball, Sermon, October 23, 1853 as found in Mark L. Staker, *Hearken, O Ye People* (Salt Lake City: Greg Kofford Books, 2009, 370).

38. *History of the Church* 1:263.

39. Writing to his brother William following a altercation between the two of them, Joseph alluded to an injury in his side that William had exacerbated that he had received during the tar and feathering. "Having once fallen in to the hands of a mob and wounded in my side, and now into the hands of a brother, my side gave way" (Dean Jessee, ed., *The Papers of Joseph Smith: Autobiographical and Historical Writings,* (Salt Lake City, UT: Deseret Book Company, 2002, 2) 116 as found in Mark L. Staker, *Hearken, O Ye People* (Salt Lake City: Greg Kofford Books, 2009), 370.

all of this, Joseph's words and great courage in proceeding with his responsibility to preach so affected the congregation that three listeners chose to be baptized and Joseph performed the ordinances that day. One of the converts was Philemon Duzette, who had passed by the Johnsons' home when the tar was being removed from Joseph's skin and took the mobbing as a sign of the validity of Joseph's calling.

Adding to the grief and heartache of the tar and feathering was the fact that on the night of the attack young Joseph Murdock Smith, who was suffering from the effects of measles, "received a severe cold, and continued to grow worse" until tragically six days later he died on Friday March 30th." This made Emma the fourth victim of the tar and feathering and was the fourth child she lost in the first five years of her marriage to Joseph.[40]

Before the attack, Joseph and Sidney had planned a trip to Missouri (see Doctrine and Covenants 78:9) so Joseph and company left the Johnsons' home on 1 April. However, concerned over the safety of Emma and Julia, he wrote her a letter suggesting that she go to Kirtland and stay with the Whitneys. When Joseph returned from Missouri he found Emma "very disconsolate."[41] Unbeknown to him, opposition from Ann Whitney's Aunt Sarah forced Emma and Julia to seek temporary living quarters with Reynolds Cahoon, Joseph's father and mother, and Frederick G. Williams.

The Johnsons were not idle during these events. After Joseph was taken out of the home, some of the mobbers remained behind, surrounding the house in order to keep those inside from coming to his aid. These mobbers fled when John Johnson threatened to shoot them if they didn't let him out despite the fact the rifles were useless. He grabbed a club and ran down the road until he came upon Sidney's body. He knocked one man down and moved toward another until several other mobbers appeared and chased him back toward his home. Another Johnson house guest, John Poorman, also joined the fray. Unfortunately, in the dark, he mistook John for a mobber

---

40. History, 1838–1856, volume A-1 [23 December 1805–30 August 1834], The Joseph Smith Papers, 3 November 2018, josephsmithpapers.org/paper-summary/history-1838–1856–volume-a-1–23–december-1805–30–august-1834/215.

41. Ibid.

and clubbed him, breaking his collarbone. Then fearing for his own safety, John Poorman ran and hid in the corn crib. When he felt it was safe to come out, he discovered he had clubbed John Johnson, who, amazingly, was instantly healed when David Whitmer administered to him.[42]

Following Joseph's departure to Missouri, the mobbers "continued to molest and menace Father Johnson's house for a long time."[43] There was little public outcry and no one was arrested, but there is some evidence that John Johnson's pursuit of civil legal action produced some minimal justice.

Other than the temporary absence of the Prophet and his family from Hiram, the mobbing did little to influence the resolve of most of the Saints in and around Hiram to remain true to the gospel. Those planning to gather to Missouri remained committed, and the first departures commenced on 2 May, eventuating in the migration of about one hundred. Most of the remaining Saints eventually moved closer to Kirtland, but a few remained in Portage County. Joseph was not deterred from returning to the Johnson Home. Upon his return from Missouri, Joseph joined his family in Kirtland temporarily, and all three moved back to Hiram at the beginning of July, where they remained until 12 September 1832, exactly one year after their arrival, when they moved back to Kirtland to live in the Whitney store.

The litany of persecution of the Prophet and Emma began when he first told a Methodist preacher in New York in 1820 about his vision of the Father and the Son and continued until he was murdered in Carthage, Illinois, in 1844. The tar and feathering added to the difficulties and sacrifices that Joseph and Emma were asked to endure for years. In fact, Emma was aware of the persecution that had commenced in the Harmony, Pennsylvania, area before her marriage to Joseph that was precipitated by the knowledge

---

42. Luke Johnson, "History of Luke Johnson," *Millennial Star* 26(53) (December 31, 1864), 835.
43. "History, 1838–1856, volume A-1 [23 December 1805–30 August 1834]," p. 209, The Joseph Smith Papers, 30 October 2018, josephsmithpapers.org/paper-summary/history-1838–1856–volume-a-1–23–december-1805–30–august-1834/215.

that had been noised about the area regarding his seeing an angel. Those who engaged in the persecution included her uncle, Nathaniel Lewis, who eventually became a chief instigator. Thus, when she accepted his marriage proposal, she was accepting a life of sacrifice, filled with potential persecution. Despite all of this, she remained faithful to her husband and continued to bear testimony of his divine calling throughout her life. Their commitment to the Restoration was absolute.

CHRONOLOGICAL SUMMARY

1–12 Nov. 1831: Several conferences—publishing revelations

4 Dec. 1831: Newell K. Whitney as bishop, bishop's duties in Kirtland (section 72)

16 Feb. 1832: The Vision (section 76)

1 Mar. 1832: United Firm in Kirtland (section 78)

24 Mar. 1832: Tar and feathering, Joseph Smith preaches the day after

1 Apr. 1832: Joseph Smith's second trip to Missouri, Emma goes to Kirtland

Mid-Apr. 1832: Arrival in Missouri

26 Apr. 1832: United Firm, sustaining as President of the High Priesthood in Missouri (section 82)

30 Apr. 1832: Widows and orphans in Missouri (section 83)

Mid-June 1832: Joseph Smith, Newell K. Whitney return from Missouri (others return sooner)

Chapter 10

"Newel K. Whitney Is the Man"

A Second Bishop, the Law of Consecration, and The United Firm: Doctrine and Covenants 72, 78, 82, and 83

Sections 72, 78, 82, and 83 of the Doctrine and Covenants represent key components in a series of revelations that began in Harmony, Pennsylvania, and continued through Fayette, New York, three different locations in Ohio, and in Missouri. They manifest the Lord's concern for the poor and the responsibility the Saints have to care for them. Although sections 72 and 78 were received in the Whitneys' home in Kirtland and 82 and 83 were received in Jackson County, Missouri, they were revealed during the period the Johnsons' home was the Prophet and Emma's residence and therefore receive treatment in this volume.

EARLY REVELATIONS

In the early stages of the revelatory downpouring that characterized the Bible translation, the Prophet learned that the people of Enoch were called Zion "because they were of one heart and one mind, and dwelt in righteousness; and there was no poor among them" (Moses 7:18). On 30 December, a month after this revelation about Enoch was received, the Lord directed the New York Saints to "go to the Ohio" (D&C 37:1). When He reiterated that command three days later in the revelation now known as section 38, he expressed an immediate concern for those "that have farms that cannot be sold" (verse 37) before they moved "to the place which I have commanded them" (verse 35), and directed "that certain men among them shall be appointed . . . to look to the poor and the needy" (verses 34–35). He also revealed principles that undergirded the specific details of his plan for caring for the temporal needs of the Saints which included "the riches of the earth are mine to give," "every man [should] esteem his brother as himself" (verse 24), "all flesh is mine" (verse 10) and thus he is "no respecter of persons" (vs. 10). and administer to their relief" (verse 35). Section 42 initiated a string of revelations regarding care for the poor later revealed in Kirtland and Hiram, Ohio and Jackson County, Missouri with ". . . thou wilt remember the poor, and consecrate of thy properties for their support" (verse 30).

REVELATIONS IN KIRTLAND AND MISSOURI PRIOR TO THE JOHNSON HOME YEAR

John Whitmer was sent to Kirtland a few weeks before Joseph and Emma. When he arrived, he discovered that many of those who had been baptized in November (see chapter 1) were attempting, under the direction of Sidney Rigdon, to follow the scriptural injunction to have "all things in common" (Acts 4:32). These new converts lived on the farm of Isaac and Lucy Morley where literally all property was held jointly by the community and was referred to as "common stock." In his role as church historian, John wrote: "The disciples had all things common, and were going to destruction very fast as to temporal things; for they considered from reading the scripture that what belonged to a brother, belonged to any of the brethren. Therefore they would take each other's clothes and other property and use it without leave which brought on confusion and disappointments, for they did not understand the scripture."[1]

Speaking of these "strange notions" after his arrival in Kirtland, Joseph wrote: "With a little caution and some wisdom, I soon assisted the brethren and sisters to overcome them. The plan of 'common stock,' which had existed in what was called 'the family,' whose members generally had embraced the everlasting Gospel, was readily abandoned for the more perfect law of the Lord."[2]

Shortly after moving in with the Newel and Ann Whitney on about 1 February, the Prophet received the first Kirtland revelation on 4 February which directed that Edward Partridge be called as the first bishop (see D&C 41:9). The revealing of the "law," now section 42, in Kirtland a few days later fulfilled the promise also given in section 38 wherein the Lord said he would "give unto [them] my law" (verse 32) if they obeyed the command to "go to the Ohio" (verse 32). The promised law (section 42) included the law of consecration, or the law of consecration and stewardship, which was to replace the common stock system—"Thou shalt not take thy brother's garment; thou shalt pay for that which thou shalt receive of thy brother" (verse 54). Edward was directed to assume responsibility for two aspects of this law—the supervision of property transactions and the consecration and resultant redistribution of personal property as the Saints were provided with stewardships (see also D&C 51).

The Lord indicated that properties were to be consecrated to the Church "with a covenant and a deed which cannot be broken" (D&C 42:30), a legally binding document entered into by a church member and by the bishop acting as the Lord's authorized agent (see D&C 42:31). After deeding all of his or

---

1. John Whitmer, History, 1831–circa 1847. *The Joseph Smith Papers*, josephsmith papers.org/paper-summary/john-whitmer-history-1831–circa-1847 /15#XEF1DE185–A6DE-4951–8045–D2CA2C1AEFB2.

2. History, 1838–1856, volume A-1 [23 December 1805–30 August 1834]. The Joseph Smith Papers. josephsmithpapers.org/paper-summary/history -1838–1856–volume-a-1–23–december-1805–30–august-1834/99#historical -intro.

her property to the Church the member received another legal, signed document from the bishop listing the personal and real estate properties that were being leased back to him, making him "a steward over his own property or that which he has received by consecration, as much as is sufficient for himself and family" (D&C 42:32). The remaining surplus obtained from initial consecrations by those who had more property than was necessary for their needs as well as from further consecrations obtained by producing more than those needs in the future was to "be kept in my storehouse, to administer to the poor and the needy, . . . and for the purpose of purchasing lands for the public benefit of the church, and building houses of worship, and building up of the New Jerusalem which is hereafter to be revealed" (D&C 42:34–35).

After Joseph, Edward, and several other brethren (see D&C 52:24) arrived in Missouri in 14 July 1831 they were informed that Jackson County was to be the New Jerusalem (Zion; see D&C 57:1–3) and Edward was to be the bishop in Zion (see D&C 58:14). Church members began gathering there in August 1831, and in early 1832, Sidney Gilbert and Newel K. Whitney, who were partners in N. K. Whitney & Co. in Kirtland, were directed to "establish a store" in Independence (D&C 57:9). It was to be operated by Sidney under the name of Gilbert and Whitney so that the Church could receive "money to buy lands for the good of the Saints" while Newel was directed to assist in this endeavor by operating his Kirtland store. These two stores constituted the beginning of the mercantile endeavors of the Church.

REVELATIONS DURING THE PROPHET AND EMMA'S RESIDENCE IN HIRAM

In addition to caring for the poor, the publication of the Prophet's revelations also required funding. On 12 November 1831, during the fourth of a series of four conferences in Hiram that began 1 November, Joseph, Oliver Cowdery, John Whitmer, and Sidney Rigdon were given the responsibility of managing the "sacred writings" of the Church. In the spirit of the law of consecration and stewardship, a revelation directed these four men along with Martin Harris and William W. Phelps be ordained "stewards over the revelations & commandments" in forming a "Literary Firm" that would provide support for them along with additional resources to be placed in the Lord's storehouse to benefit "the inhabitants of Zion & . . . their generations" (D&C 70:8; historically, the word "firm" meant "business").

FOUR REVELATIONS IN KIRTLAND AND MISSOURI

Section 72

These foregoing revelations laid the groundwork for the 4 December 1831 instructions now recorded in section 72, the related instructions revealed in section 78 the following March, and sections 82 and 83 received a month later. In the same set of conferences during which the Literary Firm was established, the Lord had indicated "in the due time of the Lord, other [would] bishops to be set apart unto the church (D&C 68:14; see chapter 8).

In introducing section 72 that discusses bishops and their responsibilities, the Prophet indicated that fulfilling the direction in section 71 to preach in the Hiram area necessitated a thirty-one–mile trip north to Kirtland-to discuss "temporal welfare."

> Knowing now the mind of the Lord, that the time had come that the Gospel should be proclaimed in power and demonstration to the world, . . . I took a journey to Kirtland, in company with Elder Sidney Rigdon on the 3rd day of December, to fulfil the above revelation. On the 4th, several of the Elders and members assembled together to learn their duty, and for edification, and after some time had been spent in conversing about our temporal and spiritual welfare, I received the following.[3]

---

3. History, 1838–1856, volume A-1 [23 December 1805–30 August 1834]. The Joseph Smith Papers.

This assemblage occurred in the home of Newel K. and Ann Whitney. Although the law of consecration was practiced differently in Kirtland than it was in Missouri, the group recognized while discussing "temporal and spiritual welfare" that there was a need for another bishop to replace Bishop Partridge in directing the regulation of stewardships and the associated care for the poor in Kirtland. Their prayers resulted in two revelations being given that same day; they are now compiled into section 72. The Lord agreed that "it [was] expedient in me for a bishop to be appointed unto you," and complimented the in that they had "done wisely" (verses 2–3).

He then indicated the new bishop was to be sustained by "the voice of the conference" and identified him "as my servant Newel K. Whitney . . . who shall be appointed and ordained unto this power" (verse 8).

Newel's grandson, the Apostle Orson F. Whitney, later wrote "The thought of assuming this important responsibility was almost more than he could bear. . . . (He) distrusted his ability, and deemed himself incapable of discharging the high and holy trust. In his perplexity he appealed to the Prophet:

> "I cannot see a Bishop in myself, Brother Joseph; but if you say it's the Lord's will, I'll try."
>
> "You need not take my word alone," answered the Prophet, kindly; "go and ask Father for yourself."
>
> Newel retired to his bedroom to seek confirmation and "heard a voice from heaven: Thy strength is in me." He then returned to the group and accepted the calling at which time he was ordained.[4]

(The revelation directing Edward to serve as the Bishop of Zion, section 57, also directed—in verse 18—that he was to be assisted by his counselors, Isaac Morley and John Corrill, who were appointed in June 1831, five months after Edward's appointment. Because these two brethren were also directed to move to Missouri, all three Kirtland

---

4. Orson F. Whitney, "The Aaronic Priesthood," *The Contributor*, January 1885, 126.

bishopric positions were vacant, resulting in the calling of Newel, followed by the call for Hyrum Smith and Reynolds Cahoon to serve as Newel's counselors in February 1832, two months following section 72). While reviewing fundamental principles relating to the role of a bishop in the law of consecration, verses 9–26, which were revealed later on the same day as verses 1–8, the Lord described the duties of the bishop in Kirtland and that they were to "be an ensample for all the extensive branches of my church, in whatsoever land they shall be established" (verse 23).

In repeating what He has said elsewhere—"the law which has been given" (D&C 42, 51)—the Lord opened section 72 by alluding to two aspects of the law of consecration that related specifically to the bishop—operating a bishop's storehouse to care for the poor and administering the consecration and redistribution of personal property. Bishops were to make inspired judgments as they "take an account of the elders (their people) as before has been commanded" in seeking "to administer to their wants," always seeking to promote self-reliance that enables their people to "pay for that which they receive" (verse 11). Eventually, the self-reliance that enabled them to "have wherewith to pay" (verse 11) could then in turn be "consecrated to the good of the church, to the poor and needy" (verse 12).

The Bishop of Zion was to utilize his resources in supporting the welfare work of local bishops, particularly when the latter's resources were insufficient to meet local welfare needs. This relationship between the local Bishop of Kirtland and the general Church Bishop of Zion was to be an "ensample" (example) for all such relationships.

This system also allowed for caring for the needs of general leaders of the Church, "who labor in spiritual things, in administering the gospel and the things of the kingdom unto the church, and unto the world" (verse 14). Similarly, those "appointed as stewards over the literary concerns of my church" (the Literary Firm discussed in section 70) "have claim for assistance upon the bishop or bishops in all things" (verse 20). This stewardship ensured "that the revelations may be published, and go forth unto the ends of the earth," that these stewards "may obtain funds which shall benefit the church in all things" (verse 21), and that they "also may render themselves approved in all things, and be accounted as wise stewards" (verse 22). The Lord also directed that the migration of Saints from Kirtland to Zion was to be conducted to ensure that worthy or "acceptable" stewards will be its citizens. They were to be "appointed by the Holy Spirit" and "carry up unto the bishop a certificate from three elders of the church, or a certificate from the bishop" (verses 24 and 25).

Section 78

On 1 March 1832, another meeting of high priests met in the Whitney home. The Lord revealed there was to "be an organization of my people, in regulating and establishing the affairs of the storehouse . . . both in this place and in the land of Zion" (D&C 78:3). Before being revised to its current wording in the 1835 edition of the Doctrine and Covenants, this verse called for an organization of "the literary and mercantile establishments of my church."[5] The brethren were directed to organize another, mercantile firm, in addition to the Literary Firm. The work of both firms was to be coordinated and become part of the church storehouse. It was referred to as the United Firm, the United Order, or the Order of Enoch. Just as the Literary Firm was governed by the law of consecration and stewardship, the members of the United Firm, which eventually numbered about twelve men, were appointed stewards over Church property and buildings to which they were given legal title and related responsibilities. The needs and wants of firm members were to be financed from revenues generated by these holdings, and surpluses were used to fund Church operations, publications, and land purchases in Zion and Kirtland. About a year later, Joseph wrote, "The order of the Literary Firm is a matter of stewardship, which is of the greatest importance; and the mercantile establishment

---

5. Revelation, 1 March 1832 [D&C 78]. The Joseph Smith Papers. josephsmith-papers.org/paper-summary/revelation-1–march-1832–dc-78/1.

God commanded to be devoted to the support thereof."[6] This initial organization was to set a pattern—"Behold, this is the preparation wherewith I prepare you, and the foundation, and the ensample which I give unto you" (verse 13)—for future such business endeavors.

Later that March, the Lord spoke on the same subject in an unpublished revelation,[7] much of which seems to reiterate the instructions provided in sections 41, 42, 70, and 78. Specific commonalities include being equal in earthly things, participating in the law of consecration by bond and covenant, regulating storehouses and their surpluses, and directing bishops to separate themselves from their personal businesses while serving as judges. It does, however, provide a unique reminder that storehouse goods are the property of the Church and not the bishop, alluding at least to Newell K. Whitney who maintained the storehouse in his mercantile. Despite an unparalleled level of service and sacrifice, Newell may not have obeyed this direction to separate "from (the) care of business" completely, at least not at first.

Sections 82 and 83

In section 78 the Lord indicated that the United Firm was to consist of Joseph Smith, Sidney Rigdon, and Newel K Whitney and that they were to "sit in council with the saints which are in Zion" (verse 9). Just one week following the horrific tar and feathering these three men, accompanied by Peter Whitmer Jr. and Jesse Gause, left Kirtland on 1 April and arrived on the 24th intending to establish a branch of the United Firm in Missouri according to the Lord's command (see Doctrine and Covenants 78:9).

---

6. History, 1838–1856, volume A-1 [23 December 1805–30 August 1834]. *The Joseph Smith Papers.*
7. "Revelation, between circa 8 and circa 24 March 1832," *The Joseph Smith Papers,* josephsmithpapers.org/paper-summary/revelation-between-circa-8-and-circa-24-march-1832/1#historical-intro.

During the 26 April council meeting of leading brethren from Missouri and Ohio, Joseph was sustained as president of the high priesthood as he had previously been in Amherst, Ohio (15 January 1832). The council then dealt with a contention between Sidney Rigdon and Edward Partridge that stemmed from a September 1831 letter in which Sidney charged Edward with disparaging the Prophet. The two were able to settle their differences after which the Lord himself responded in the revelation recorded in section 82: "Inasmuch as you have forgiven one another your trespasses, even so I, the Lord, forgive you" (verse 1). Then He warned the council "to beware from henceforth, and refrain from sin" (verse 2) because "for of him unto whom much is given much is required; and he who sins against the greater light shall receive the greater condemnation. . . . I, the Lord, am bound when ye do what I say; but when ye do not what I say, ye have no promise" (verses 3 and 10).

The Lord then directed that the members of the Literary Firm were to be "bound together" in the United Firm and were to be joined by Bishop Edward Partridge "to manage the affairs of the poor, and all things pertaining to the bishopric both in the land of Zion and in the land of Kirtland" (verses 11 and 12), reminding the brethren that although Zion was to be the central gathering place, Kirtland was to be "a strong hold . . . for the space of five years" (D&C 54:21). The original revealed language highlighted the historical context—"to manage the literary & Mercantile concerns & the Bishopricks both in the Land of Zion & in the Land of Kirtland."[8]

The Lord then directed the members of the firm to create legally binding contracts with each other "according to the laws of the land" (verse 15) and reiterated that it provided stewardships for brethren who served full time in the Church, enabling their temporal needs to be met, "every man according to his wants and his needs" (verse 17).

The day after section 82 was revealed, the members of the United Firm met again and decided that the two mercantile components of the United Firm would be named Gilbert, Whitney &

---

8. Revelation, Independence, Jackson Co., MO [D&C 82]. *The Joseph Smith Papers.* josephsmithpapers.org/paper-summary/revelation-26–april-1832–dc-82/1

Company in Zion and Newel K. Whitney & Company in Kirtland Geauga Co. Ohio. At the meeting on 30 April of the United Firm, the revelation now known as section 83 was revealed and made special mention of the need to care for widows and children. It was further "Resolved That the firm [secure a] loan [of] fifteen thousand dollars for five years or longer at six per cent annually or semi-annually as the agreement can be made, & that N.K. Whitney & Co. be appointed to negotiate the same."[9] Newel assumed responsibility for this debt and acquired a combination of loans from business contacts in Buffalo, New York.[10]

During the following two years, the United Firm directed the two mercantiles (storehouses), the printing office, and other ventures. The assets derived from their operation provided financing for various church projects and for living expenses of members of the firm and their families. In 1833, the Lord directed that two other brethren be added to the firm. Jesse Gause was named as a member of the firm, and the Lord said in March that his replacement in the First Presidency, Frederick G. Williams, was to be received "into the firm" and be "a lively member" (D&C 92:1–2). In June, he also directed that John Johnson "become a member of the firm that he may assist in bringing forth my word unto the children of men." (D&C 96:8). Both of these brethren owned large properties that were added to the resources of the firm in consecration.

Unfortunately, Missouri persecutions weakened the financial foundations of the United Firm. Both the Gilbert store and the Phelps printing office had provided critical resources that were lost when the Saints were driven out of Jackson County in the summer and fall of 1833. Further debt-related financial constraints stemmed from securing the loans to purchase storehouse goods, acquiring a new printing press in Kirtland to replace the press that was destroyed

---

9.   Minutes, circa 1 May 1832. The Joseph Smith Papers. josephsmithpapers.org/paper-summary/minutes-circa-1–may-1832/1
10. Mark Lyman Staker, *Hearken O Ye People: The Historical Setting of Joseph Smith's Ohio Revelations* (Salt Lake City: Greg Kofford Books, 2009), 231.

by the Missouri mob, and purchasing land for further development of Kirtland.

Newel K. Whitney was also designated a "lively member" of the firm. Besides operating his Kirtland store as a storehouse, he used it to provide support for Joseph and others. He also consecrated his lands and his lucrative ashery operation, assumed responsibility for the debts associated with acquiring the French farm where the temple was to be built,[11] and loaned Joseph, Oliver, and Sidney a total of $3,600. The other members of the firm were not unsympathetic to Newel's difficult financial situation. Five of them joined him on 11 January 1834 to offer up their united prayers that the Lord "would provide, in the order of his Providence, the bishop of this Church with means sufficient to discharge every debt that the Firm owes, in due season."[12] However, by April, Newel's indebtedness totaled $8,000, of which $4,000 was due that month and the balance by September.[13] On 10 April, Joseph led a meeting of the firm where the brethren decided that "the firm should be desolvd and each one have their stewardship set off to them."[14]

That same month, the Lord revealed in what is now known as section 104 that the stewardships directed by the firm (specific properties) would be assigned to firm members. Newel's houses, store, his properties and ashery were returned to him. Others were given parcels of the land and buildings owned by Frederick G. Williams and John Johnson. Newel also noted that "Joseph said it was the will of the Lord" that the accounts be balanced "in full without any value rec[eived],"[15] so Newel forgave the $3,600

11. Geauga Co., Ohio, Deed Records, 1795–1921, vol. 17, 360–61, microfilm 20,237, U.S. and Canada Record Collection, Family History Library, Salt Lake City.

12. Prayer, 11 January 1834. *The Joseph Smith Papers*. josephsmithpapers.org/paper-summary/prayer-11–january-1834/1

13. Order from Newel K. Whitney, 18 April 1834. The Joseph Smith Papers. josephsmithpapers.org/paper-summary/order-from-newel-k-whitney-18–april-1834/1

14. Journal, 1832–1834. *The Joseph Smith Papers*. josephsmithpapers.org/paper-summary/journal-1832–1834/73

15. Balance of Account, 23 April 1834. *The Joseph Smith Papers*. josephsmithpapers.org/paper-summary/balance-of-account-23–april-1834/1

owed him by Joseph, Oliver, and Sidney, showing his willingness to follow the Prophet without any bitterness, even in temporal matters. Although this revelation did not call for it, the firm more or less ceased functioning at that point, and the Kirtland High Council that had been formed two months prior directed mercantile and publishing enterprises.[16]

16. Max H Parkin, "Joseph Smith and the United Firm: The Growth and Decline of the Church's First Master Plan of Business and Finance, Ohio and Missouri, 1832–1834," *BYU Studies*, 46, no. 3 (2007): 33–34.

CHRONOLOGICAL SUMMARY

Chapter 11

"A Transcript from the Records of the Eternal Worlds"

The Vision and Book of Revelation Interpretation— Doctrine and Covenants 76 and 77

The southwest, second story bedroom of the Johnson Home that served as the Prophet's office has been made sacred by the numerous revelations received there. This is especially true when one considers the grand revelation Joseph and Sidney Rigdon received on 12 February 1832. In this vision they witnessed the Savior, Lucifer, perdition, the three degrees of glory, and other divine manifestations. If the only revelation the Prophet ever received was this vision, it alone would be sufficient to bear witness of the divinity of his calling.

EVENTS LEADING UP TO THE VISION

Joseph was first sustained as president of the high priesthood at a conference in Amherst, Ohio, three weeks before the vision was revealed, during which he also received two revelations that are now recorded in section 75. He referenced these experiences in his introduction to the vision as he described the doctrinal conversation he and Sidney had regarding heaven and hell. This conversation led to the conclusion "that many important points touching the salvation of man had been taken from the Bible, or lost before it was compiled," including the notion that "if God rewarded every one according to the deeds done in the body the term 'Heaven,' as intended for the Saints' eternal home, must include more kingdoms than one" (heading, Doctrine and Covenants 76). Sidney's Reformed Baptist associate, Alexander Campbell, had taught the concept of three kingdoms as early as 1828, along with the specific requirements associated for entrance into each one.[1] Sidney was highly influenced by Alexander and his teachings in this regard and may have played an additional role in Joseph and Sidney's premise that heaven "must include more kingdoms than one."[2]

A few of the introductory verses of section 76 continue the narrative. As implied by the section heading, the conversations between Joseph and Sidney, and possibly other brethren, that preceded the vision occurred "while (they) were doing the work of translation of "the fifth chapter of John" which taught of only two conditions that follow the judgment—the resurrection of life and of damnation They were then surprised that the inspiration dictating the translation seemed to leave the basic "heaven or hell" perspective intact, leading to further conversation during which "the Lord touched the eyes of our understandings and they were opened, and the glory of the Lord shone round about" (verse 19).

THE VISIONARY EXPERIENCE

What is known about the role the men in the room played is due in large measure to the meticulous journal writing of Philo Dibble, whose reminisces appear in two accounts. In one he described what approximately twelve other men, including himself, did and did not see.

---

1.   Alexander Campbell, *The Christian Baptist,* no. 11 (1 June 1829): 557–559.
2.   Emanuel Swedenborg, a noted eighteenth century Swedish mystic, nobleman and scientist, may have also directly or indirectly influenced Joseph and Sidney's conversation (see Emanuel Swedenborg, Heaven and Hell. 1758, translator John C. Alger, 1900, #29 sacred-texts.com/swd/hh/hh01.htm See also J. B. Haws, "Joseph Smith, Emanuel Swedenborg, and section 76: Importance of the Bible in Latter-day Revelation," *The Doctrine and Covenants: Revelations in Context*, eds. Andrew H. Hedges, J. Spencer Fluhman & Alonzo L. Gaskill, 142–167 rsc.byu.edu/book/doctrine-covenants-revelations-context).

> During the time that Joseph and Sidney were in the spirit and saw the heavens open . . . not a sound nor motion made by anyone but Joseph and Sidney, and it seemed to me that they never moved a joint or limb during the time I was there. . . . I saw the glory and felt the power, but did not see the vision.[3]

In another account, Philo recorded their appearance "Joseph wore black clothes, but at this time seemed to be dressed in an element of glorious white, and his face shone as if it were transparent, but I did not see the same glory attending Sidney."[4] Joseph's transfiguration was not an occurrence limited exclusively to this vision. Numerous accounts document that like others,[5] a change in the Prophet's appearance frequently accompanied his reception of revelation (see chapter 5).

Two recollections indicate differing estimates of the time required for the vision to unfold. Philo indicated the time he spent witnessing Joseph and Sidney was a little over an hour and constituted two-thirds of the total,[6] while Sidney recalled "we sat for hours in the Visions of heaven around the throne of God & gazed upon the seenes of Eternity."[7] This apparent contradiction may perhaps be understood when it is remembered that Philo was only in the room for part of the time the vision was unfolded and that Joseph and Sidney were commanded to "write while in the spirit" several times. Philo's estimate possibly reflects the length of time the vision itself was seen, whereas Sidney's may reflect the time spent in the vision and time spent recording it.

---

3. Philo Dibble, "Recollections of the Prophet Joseph Smith," *Juvenile Instructor*, 27 no.10 (May 1892): 303–304.
4. Philo Dibble, "Philo Dibble's Narrative," in *Early Scenes in Church History, Faith-Promoting Series 8* (Salt Lake City, UT: Juvenile Instructor's Office, 1882) 81.
5. Others, including the Savior (Matthew 17:2), Moses (Exodus 34:29; Moses 1:11), Enoch (Moses 7:3); Abinadi (Mosiah 13:5), Nephi and Lehi (Helaman 5:36), and the Nephite disciples (3 Nephi 19:35) all experienced transfiguration in a like manner.
6. Philo Dibble, "Recollections of the Prophet Joseph Smith."
7. Journal, December 1842–June 1844; Book 4, 1 March–22 June 1844, note 120. The Joseph Smith Papers. josephsmithpapers.org/paper-summary/journal-december-1842–june-1844–book-4–1–march-22–june-1844/63#full-transcript

Joseph and Sidney continued their pre-vision conversation as the vision itself was unfolded, again described by Philo. "Joseph would, at intervals, say: 'What do I see' as one might say while looking out the window and beholding what all in the room could not see. Then he would relate what he had seen or what he was looking at. Then Sidney replied, 'I see the same.' Presently Sidney would say 'what do I see?' and would repeat what he had seen or was seeing, and Joseph would reply, 'I see the same.'"[8]

Remarkably, they also testified there was a third participant in the conversation that occurred between Joseph and Sidney while the vision was being revealed, even "Jesus Christ, who is the Son, whom we saw and with whom we conversed in the heavenly vision (D&C 76:14). There are at least seven separate verses in section 76 that clearly describe what the Savior said while leading this conversation (see verses 5, 31, 40, 49, 80, 110, and 115).

Philo also contrasted Joseph and Sidney's appearance during the vision. "Joseph appeared as strong as a lion, but Sidney seemed as weak as water, and Joseph, noticing his condition smiled and said, 'Brother Sidney is not as used to it as I am."[9] Elsewhere, Philo added , "Joseph sat firmly and calmly all the time in the midst of a magnificent glory, but Sidney sat limp and pale, apparently as limber as a rag."[10]

THE VISION ITSELF

Although Joseph called this revelation the "Vision," section 76 is actually a record of a series of visions. First, there was a vision of the Father and the Son (see verses 14–24); next, a vision of the premortal world and the of the fall of Satan (see verses 25–49); and visions of the celestial (see verses 50–70), terrestrial (see verses71–80), and the telestial kingdoms (see verses 81–89), respectively. These visions are followed by a comparison of the three kingdoms, which may also have been revealed through a vision, or perhaps may be verbiage uttered by the Prophet and Sidney as they were moved upon by the Holy Ghost.

---

8. Philo Dibble, "Recollections of the Prophet Joseph Smith."
9. Philo Dibble, "Philo Dibble's Narrative,"
10. Philo Dibble, "Recollections of the Prophet Joseph Smith."

A Vision of the Father and the Son

The privilege of seeing the Savior has already been mentioned (see verse 14), but Joseph and Sidney actually saw two beings, "the Son, on the right hand of the Father," who also bore "record that he is the Only Begotten of the Father" (verse 23) and possessed the dual roles of Creator and Savior (see verse 24).[11]

The privilege of seeing deity in the Kirtland area was not confined exclusively to the Johnson Home. The Prophet was privileged to see the Father and the Son at least six other times—on the Morley farm on   June 1831 when the first high priests of this dispensation were ordained,[12] in the Whitney Store on 18 March 1833 when the First Presidency was fully constituted,[13] and at least four times in the Kirtland Temple in January 1836 when the initiatory ordinances were first performed in our dispensation.[14] He probably also saw the Savior an additional three or four times—in the John Johnson Inn (in Kirtland) on 18 December 1833 when Joseph was providing blessings for his parents,[15] three times in the temple in connection with the initiatory ordinances,[16] once on 30 March 1836 during the solemn assembly,[17] and on 7 April 1836 when the Savior appeared and accepted the Kirtland Temple (see Doctrine and Covenants 110).

---

11. Russell M. Nelson, October 1996 general conference, lds.org/general -conference/1996/10/the-atonement?lang=eng.
12. "Levi Hancock, Journal," Special Collections, Harold B. Lee Library, Brigham Young University, Provo, UT.
13. Minutes, 18 March 1833, *The Joseph Smith Paper*s. josephsmithpapers. org/paper-summary/minutes-18–march-1833/2; Minutes, 18 March 1833, notes 12 & 13. The Joseph Smith Papers. josephsmithpapers.org/transcript/ minutes-18–march-1833?print=true
14. Doctrine and Covenants 137:1–3; Orson F. Whitney, *Life of Heber C. Kimball* (Salt Lake City, UT: Juvenile Instructor's Office, 1888), 68; 1835– 1836, The Joseph Smith Papers. josephsmithpapers.org/paper-summary/ journal-1835–1836/146
15. Appendix 5: Blessings, September and October 1835, Introduction, The Joseph Smith Papers. josephsmithpapers.org/paper-summary/appendix-5– blessings-september-and-october-1835–introduction/1
16. Journal, 1835–1836, The Joseph Smith Papers. josephsmithpapers.org/ paper-summary/journal-1835–1836/146
17. Journal, 1835–1836, The Joseph Smith Papers. josephsmithpapers.org/ paper-summary/journal-1835–1836/192

Of all these appearances, the one that occurred in the Johnson Home stands out in a unique way because it was the first such appearance that was published—in the July 1832 *The Evening and Morning Star*, which was published in Missouri. The two appearances of the Father and the Son that occurred prior to section 76, the First Vision in 1820, and the appearance on the Morley farm in 1831 were not made public until several years later

The Premortal World and the Fall of Satan

The second vision seen by Joseph and Sidney concerned the premortal world. Joseph had learned of the premortal world during the Book of Mormon (see Alma 13:2–3) and Bible translations (see Moses 3:5), as well as through earlier revelations recorded in the Doctrine and Covenants (see D&C 38:1). The part of the premortal world about which the Lord commanded Joseph and Sidney to write "while . . . yet in the Spirit" (verse 28) pertained to the rebellion and fall of Lucifer who "maketh war with the saints" (verse 29) and those he had overcome. Previous revelatory experiences had likewise prepared the Prophet for the vision of the rebellion of Lucifer during the premortal existence (seee 2 Nephi 2: 17, Moses 4:1–3; D&C 29:36–37, Abraham 3:27–28).

The Three Kingdoms of Glory

After "the end of the vision of the sufferings of the ungodly" (verse 49), the Lord turned the attention of Joseph and Sidney to the post-mortal portion of His plan that described those inheritors of the three kingdoms of glory in three separate visions. He first revealed the lifestyle of and the eventual blessings given to those who will inhabit the celestial kingdom—the "just" that have lived the doctrine of Christ (verses 51–52) and have "overcome by faith" (verse 53). Having been "sealed by the Holy Spirit of Promise," they "shall come forth in the resurrection of the just" (verse 50), possess celestial bodies "whose glory is that of the sun, even the glory of God" (verse 70), and "shall dwell in the presence of God and his Christ foever and ever" (verses 53–54, 62–64).

The same pattern of depicting lifestyle and blessings, the following vision of the "terrestrial "world" described its inhabitants as honorable men . . . who were blinded by craftiness of men" (verse 75–76), "who are not valiant in the testimony of Jesus" (verse 79), " who died without law," and who "received not the testimony of Jesus in the flesh, but afterwards received it" (verses 72–74). Therefore, they "receive of the presence of the son, but not of the fulness of the Father, wherefore they are bodies terrestrial, and not bodies celestial" (verses 77–78).

The Prophet and Sidney were then shown "the glory of the telestial, which glory is that of the lesser" (verses 80–81) while also comparing the inheritors of that glory to the sons of perdition. Although "these are they who received not the gospel of Christ" (verse 82), "they deny not the Holy Spirit" (verse 83), but instead "are liars, and sorcerers, and adulterers, and whoremongers, and whosoever loves and makes a lie" (verse 103). Like perdition, "they are thrust down to hell" (verse 84) and "suffer the wrath of Almighty God" (verse 106) but shall eventually "be redeemed from the devil" albeit not "until the last resurrection" (verse 85).

These verses about the telestial kingdom represent a combination of knowledge revealed in the fifth vision as well as a kingdom comparison Joseph and Sidney either saw or composed under inspiration. That comparison also included a reiteration of some of the descriptions of the celestial kingdom as well as additional doctrine (see verses 92, 94–95).

The Savior concluded this comparison by testifying that His atoning sacrifice enables Him to "deliver up the kingdom, and present it unto the Father, spotless, saying: I have overcome and have trodden the wine-press alone, even the wine-press of the fierceness of the wrath of Almighty God. Then shall he be crowned with the crown of his glory, to sit on the throne of his power to reign forever and ever" (verses 107–108).

ANOTHER RECORD OF THE VISION

There is an additional recording of the doctrines revealed in section 76. A poem entitled "The Answer, To W. W. Phelps, esq., The Vision" with the Prophet's signature at its end appeared in the Nauvoo *Times and Seasons* in 1843.[18] In it the doctrines of the vision are re-displayed.

---

18. Poem to William W. Phelps, between circa 1 and circa 15 February 1843, *The Joseph Smith Papers.* josephsmithpapers.org/paper-summary/poem-to-william-w-phelps-between-circa-1–and-circa-15–february-1843/1 (see appendix).

The signature may signify the Prophet was the author, but it is more likely that William W. Phelps was its author and that the signature represents Joseph's involvement or at least approval. The complete poem is quite lengthy—seventy-two stanzas—but two small portions that added additional understanding are presented here. It describes the premortal council as occurring "in Kolob." It also suggests that in addition to them who are "holy angels, and them who are sanctified," are "sanctified beings from worlds that have been," "round the throne" "worshipping God and the Lamb" (stanza 17).

THE UNRECORDED PORTIONS OF THE VISION

There was a substantial portion of the Vision that Joseph and Sidney were not allowed to record. "But great and marvelous are the works of the Lord, and the mysteries of his kingdom which he showed unto us, . . . which he commanded us we should not write while we were yet inn the Spirit, and are not lawful for man to utter" (verses 114–115). This command represented a repetition of divine instruction received elsewhere. On more than one occasion Joseph was not allowed to share all he heard and saw during his communications with God. For example, although he provided in four other accounts details related to his First Vision beyond the canonized account in the Joseph Smith—History, that particular account includes this statement of omission: "And many other things did he say unto me, that I cannot write at this time" (verse 20). Likewise, Joseph explained that during each of his annual interviews with the angel Moroni, there was much information he received of which he provided little or no record "respecting what the Lord was going to do, and how and in what manner his kingdom was to be conducted in the last days "(JS—H 1:54). Eleven years later on 21 May 1843, the Prophet suggested the size of the unrecorded portions of the Vision. "I could explain a hundred-fold more than I ever have of the glories of the kingdoms manifested to me in the vision, were I permitted, and were the people prepared to receive them."[19]

---

19. History, 1838–1856, volume D-1 [1 August 1842–1 July 1843], The Joseph Smith Papers. josephsmithpapers.org/paper-summary/history-1838–1856–volume-d-1–1–august-1842–1–july-1843/199

PROCLAIMING THE VISION AND VARIED RESPONSES TO IT

Despite his initial counsel to restrict sharing it broadly, records of the Vision were soon copied by hand and carried throughout the Church, and many rejoiced in its portrayal of the plan of salvation. In Independence, William W. Phelps called it "the greatest news that was ever published to man"[20] when he printed it in the *Evening and Morning Star*, and Samuel Smith quoted Lincoln Haskins in saying it consisted of "great & marvilous things."[21]

---

20. "Items for the Public," *The Evening and the Morning Star*, 1 no. 2 (July 1832), 27–30.
21. Samuel Harrison Smith Diary, 1832 February–1833 CHL. MS 4213. Revelation for Lincoln Haskins. The first of four unpublished revelations given in the Johnsons' home was received shortly after section 76 on February 27, 1832. On this date, the Saints from the Hiram area who were going to gather to "Zion," Jackson County, Missouri, had met in the Johnson Home to plan their move. In that setting, the Prophet received divine instructions indicating Lincoln Haskins was to be called to missionary service and supplied with copies of some of the revelations which he was directed to use on his mission.

    Lincoln Haskins was born in Massachusetts in 1779 just three years after the Prophet's mother, Lucy. He eventually moved himself and his family to Chautauque County, New York, the county in the northwest corner of New York just east of Erie that is 164 miles southwest of Palmyra. In February 1832, Lincoln traveled to Kirtland and was baptized on the 21st. His reasons for traveling there are unknown, but he may have heard of the Prophet in some way, possibly from missionaries. Like many others, he may have sought to meet Joseph for himself, but had to journey from Kirtland to Hiram to do so. He left for home shortly after the meeting, and Samuel Smith and Orson Hyde stopped for dinner at his home in New York by the end of March while on a mission to the east. They indicate Lincoln was an Elder which suggests he was probably ordained in Kirtland or Hiram. In fact, his ordination was dictated in the revelation as shown below. Having heard of the "Vision" while in Ohio, he expressed his enthusiasm for it during their visit. The dating of his mission call indicates he was of considerable age for missionary service—52.

    Lincoln had moved to Kirtland by 1836, probably with his family, and he moved to Lee County, Iowa after 1840 where he died. Lee County was across the Mississippi River from Nauvoo and was home to at least one hundred LDS families by the time of Lincoln's arrival. Although not all Kirtland immigrants traveled to and settled in northwestern Missouri prior to moving on Nauvoo, it is likely he

Not all, however, reacted similarly. It caused consternation among non-Latter-day Saints and, indeed, Sidney believed it was a cause of the tar and feathering he and Joseph received just a month later.[22] A number of Church members likewise struggled with it. For example, John Murdock noted the reaction of Church members in the Orange, Ohio, branch. "The brethren had just received the Revelation called the vision & were stumbling at it. I called them together & confirmed them in the truth."[23] Orson Pratt was not as fortunate when he encountered a branch president in New York who said, "The vision was of the Devil."[24] Orson was able to temporarily quiet the branch president's fears as he explained the doctrine to his congregation, but when missionaries returned to the branch that same year, the branch president and several of his members were excommunicated for their resistance to accepting the revelation. Even Brigham Young, who was known throughout his life as an ardent supporter of the Prophet, acknowledged that the Vision "was a great trial to many, and some apostatized. . . . It was a new doctrine to this generation, and many stumbled at it."[25] He then confessed to experiencing a moment of pause himself. "My traditions were such, that when the Vision came first to me, it was so directly contrary and opposed to my former education, I said, wait a little; I did not reject it, but I could not understand it." He added, "I [had] to think and pray, to read and think, until I knew and fully understood it for myself."[26] But patience paid

---

joined the Saints in their move to Missouri. If so, it is also quite possible he was a member of the "Kirtland Camp," the large group of saints who left Kirtland in the summer of 1838. The assumption that these two conjectures are true leads to a further conjecture that he and his family would have been part of the mass exodus from Missouri early in 1839 following the "Extermination Order."

22. Minutes and Discourses, 6–9 April 1844, as Reported by Thomas Bullock, The Joseph Smith Papers. josephsmithpapers.org/paper-summary/minutes-and-discourses-6–9–april-1844–as-reported-by-thomas-bullock/8

23. John Murdock, "Journal," Church History Library, The Church of Jesus Christ of Latter-day Saints, 18; spelling and punctuation have been modernized.

24. Orson Pratt, "Diaries 1833–1837," Dec. 29, 1833, Church History Library, The Church of Jesus Christ of Latter-day Saints; spelling and punctuation have been modernized.

25. Brigham Young, *Discourses of Brigham Young Selected by John A. Widtsoe* (Salt Lake City: Deseret Book Company, 1926) 598.

26. *Journal of Discourses*, 6:281.

off and he later said, "I can truly say that, in my estimation, no other revelation so glorious was ever given." [27]

The traditions to which Brigham referred reflected widely held traditional Christian beliefs in their depiction of heaven and the nature of salvation that early converts didn't necessarily have to reject in order to join the Church prior to the Vision. In at least four ways its publication presented a stark contrast. First, despite New Testament verses to the contrary and the views of Reformed Baptist leader Alexander Campbell, the notion of one heaven was cemented in the minds of most Christians.

Second, the Vision was viewed by some as an insult to the traditional Christian belief that hell was a place where the wicked suffered for eternity with no hope of escape. On the contrary, the Vision revealed that a permanent "lake of fire and brimstone" was anticipated only for the sons of perdition and the one-third of the hosts of heaven who rejected God's plan in the premortal existence, including Satan. Otherwise, hell was to be a temporary punishment for the wicked who were not guilty of sin against the Holy Ghost and was designed to cleanse them in preparation for an inheritance in a kingdom of glory.

Third, the first two differences also made plain that nearly all of God's children would receive salvation, albeit by degree, which sounded a lot like Universalism. Universalists, whose numbers included Joseph's grandfather Aasel Smith and who were a small minority in America in the years before the Restoration, believed that all mankind would be saved regardless of faith, works, or ordinances. This perspective was cause for vigorous debate among Christians because most believed that there would be a relatively sparse population in heaven and a very crowded hell. Had opponents of the doctrines portrayed in the Vision studied it more closely, they would have noted a vast difference between the Vision and Universalism. While it did provide for the redemption of nearly all of God's children, only some would enjoy a fulness of heavenly reward, and it clearly testified of the need for a Savior whose atoning sacrifice provided grace on conditions of faith, repentance, baptism, the gift of the Holy Ghost, and enduring to the end. Additionally, as mentioned above, hell was a valid concept, albeit

---

27. *Journal of Discourses*, 8:153.

temporary for most of its inhabitants and permanent for a relative few. Therefore, while revealing God as providing as much reward as His mercy and justice would allow, it also confirmed the role of man's agency in determining the nature of his afterlife.

Another possible source of opposition stemmed from Joseph and Sydney's declaration that "we saw Him, even on the right hand of God." As discussed previously, although the Prophet had seen visions of the Father and the Son prior to this vision, none of them had been published before the time of this vision, 16 February 1832. Therefore, the Vision represents the first account of the appearance of the Father and the Son to Joseph that was made public.

Despite the opposition to it from some within the Church, most members possessed a sentiment similar to that of the Prophet, and it has been echoed by millions of Latter-day Saints since 1832. "Nothing could be more pleasing to the Saints upon the order of the kingdom of the Lord, than the light which burst upon the world through the foregoing vision. Every law, every commandment, every promise, every truth, and every point touching the destiny of man, from Genesis to Revelation, where the purity of the scriptures remains unsullied by the folly of men, go to show the perfection of the theory [of different degrees of glory in the future life] and witnesses the fact that that document is a transcript from the records of the eternal world. The sublimity of the ideas; the purity of the language; the scope for action; the continued duration for completion, in order that the heirs of salvation may confess the Lord and bow the knee; the rewards for faithfulness, and the punishments for sins, are so much beyond the narrow-mindedness of men, that every honest man is constrained to exclaim: 'It came from God.'"[28]

DOCTRINE AND COVENANTS 77

Following the receipt of the Vision and the Lincoln Haskins revelation, Joseph and Sidney traveled to Kirtland on 29 February

---

28. Vision, 16 February 1832 [D&C 76], Historical Introduction, The Joseph Smith Papers, josephsmithpapers.org/paper-summary/vision-16–february-1832–dc-76/1#historical-intro

to discuss the Church's publishing and mercantile endeavors and returned to Hiram on 4 March. Joseph then recorded: "About the first of March, in connection with the translation of the scriptures, I received the following explanation of the Revelations of Saint John (D&C 77 heading)." The dating of this revelation is complex. The Prophet, or those writing his history, use an approximation of "about the first of March." Joseph had been in Kirtland from 29 February to 4 March, during which time section 78 was revealed, so it must have been revealed after 4 March 4. On the 20th, as discussed below, Joseph and Sidney were directed in section 78 to postpone further translation in favor of a second trip to Missouri. However, they were translating Revelation 11 on the day of the tar and feathering, 24 March, and that chapter is the last one treated in section 77, so it is not unreasonable to conclude 77 was revealed that day.

John the Revelator received the revelation recorded in the book of Revelation in the New Testament while exiled to the island of Patmos (see Revelation 1:9–10). Because of its rich imagery and symbolism, comprehending Revelation is often a difficult task, so Joseph directed missionaries to not teach about the book's symbols and details, but to stick to basic gospel principles.[29] However, the Prophet called this book "one of the plainest books God ever caused to be written,"[30] and section 77's fifteen inspired questions and answers make understanding some of Revelation a little less challenging by interpreting some of the symbols and events that are contained in its first eleven chapters.

---

29. Manuscript History, vol. D-1, page 1523, *The Joseph Smith Papers*, josephsmithpapers.org/paper-summary/history-1838–1856–volume-d-1–1–august-1842–1–july-1843/166.
30. Ibid.

CHRONOLOGICAL SUMMARY

1–12 Nov. 1831: several conferences—publishing revelations

11 Nov. 1831: Church government (section 107)

12 Nov. 1831: Literacy Firm (section 70)

1 Dec. 1831: Trouble with apostates, suspend JST (section 71)

~3–9 Dec. 1831: Preaching around Kirtland

4 Dec. 1831: Newell K. Whitney as bishop, bishop's duties in Kirtland (section 72)

10 Jan. 1832: Trouble assuaged, resume JST (section 73)

25 Jan. 1832: Sustaining as President of the High Priesthood, mission calls in Amherst, Ohio (section 75)

16 Feb. 1832: The Vision (section 76)

15 Mar. 1832: Gause, Williams, First Presidency (section 81)

~4–20 Mar. 1832: JST, The Book of Revelation (section 77)

Chapter 12

"The Keys Which Belong Unto the Presidency of the High Priesthood"

The Evolving Quorum of the First Presidency:
Doctrine and Covenants 81, 107, 167

Of three general leadership quorums in The Church of Jesus Christ of Latter-day Saints—the First Presidency, the Quorum of the Twelve Apostles, and the Seventy—the first to be restored was the First Presidency. Its line-upon-line restoration occurred over a two–year period, much of it while Joseph and Emma resided in the Johnsons' home. (A discussion of the Apostleship and its keys is found in the appendix.) It is a remarkable story attesting to the divine origin of the organizational structure of the Church and the revelatory calling of the Prophet Joseph Smith.

On the surface, three early revelations now recorded in sections 20 (around April 6, 1830, Fayette, New York), 48 (March 10, 1831, Kirtland, Ohio), and 68 (November 1, 1831, Hiram, Ohio) would appear to contain the initial divine directions regarding the establishment of the First Presidency. However, the wording in these sections when first revealed did not include wording relating to the First Presidency and were added under divine inspiration in 1835 as the Prophet prepared the revelations for publication. The first divine directions actually pertaining to the First Presidency appear in the second part of section 107.

TERMS WITH CHANGING DEFINITIONS

There are a few terms that appear in 107 that played an important role in the unfolding restoration whose meanings have evolved over time. Understanding the meaning of these terms enables a clearer understanding of the events corresponding to the restoration of the Quorum of the First Presidency. Also, this semantic evolution no doubt served to establish the notion that leadership in and of the priesthood equates to leadership in and of the Church.

For example, "then comes the High Priesthood" (verse 64) first referred to the office of high priest and later the Melchizedek Priesthood as in the first few verses of the current, compiled version of section 107. Therefore, "President of the High Priesthood" and "Presiding High Priest over the High Priesthood" (verses 65–66) first referred to the "President of the office of the High Priesthood" as the man who was "to preside over the whole church" (Joseph Smith, verse 91) and later president of the high priests quorum (Don Carlos Smith, the Prophet's youngest brother; the concept of stake presidents serving as the presidents of stake high priesthood quorums was not part of local church organization until the 1960s.[1])

The Prophet traveled to Amherst, Ohio, sxity-four miles west of Hiram, on 25 January to fulfill the command "that one be appointed to preside over the priesthood" (verse 65). There "the Prophet Joseph was acknowledged (sustained) President of the High Priesthood."[2] Likewise, in the "land of Zion" the Prophet "was acknowledged [sustained] President of the High Priesthood."[3]

1. W. V. Smith, *A Preliminary Historical and Critial Analysis of Doctrine and Covenants Section 107,* boap.org/LDS/Historical-Analysis-the-Doctrine-and-Covenants/An-Historical-Analysis-of-D&C-107.html.

2. Orson Pratt, "Life and Labors of Orson Pratt"—History of Orson Pratt (Written by Himself)," *The Contributor,* 12(3), 3 January 1891.

3. Minutes, 26–27 April 1832, *The Joseph Smith Papers,* josephsmithpapers.org/paper-summary/minutes-26–27–april-1832/1.

COUNSELORS TO THE PROPHET

The general notion of standing counselors began with the designation of Isaac Morley and John Corrill as counselors to Bishop Edward Partridge in June 1831 and Hyrum Smith and Reynolds Cahoon as counselors to Bishop Newel K. Whitney in February 1832. The phrase "to assist as counselors" to a president first appear in Doctrine and Covenants 107:79. Then in an unpublished revelation received probably in the middle of March 1832 the Lord said that "unto the office of the presidency of the high Priesthood I have given authority to preside with the assistence of his councellers over all the concerns of the church."[4] The term "presidency" also had two meanings. Initially, it was used to designate the prophet's office just as it is used in referring to the office of the President of the United States (for example, "Washington's presidency"). It later came to also refer to a president and her or his counselors, beginning with the creation of the First Presidency. It would be premature, however, to suggest this divine direction to select counselors would complete the evolution of the First Presidency. Rather, these counselors were to assist the Prophet, who at that point was the only one appointed to preside over the Church.

Around the time of this revelation, 8 March, Joseph selected two counselors: "Chose this day and ordained brother Jesse Gause and Broth[er] Sidney [Rigdon] to be my councillers of the ministry of the presidency of th[e] high Pristhood."[5] The Lord then provided further instructions on 15 March regarding the role of counselors—now known as section 81—supporting what He had previously said in the unpublished revelation. In its original form, it began by addressing Jesse Gause: "Verily Verily I say unto you my servant Jesse." The heading to the section explains that "the historical records show that when this revelation was received . . . , it called Jesse Gause to the office of counselor to Joseph Smith in the Presidency. However, when he failed to continue in a manner consistent with this appointment, the

---

4. Chad J. Flake, The Newel K. Whitney Collection, *Brigham Young University Studies*, 11(4), Summer 1971, 322–328.
5. "Note, 8 March 1832," *The Joseph Smith Papers*, josephsmithpapers.org/paper-summary/note-8–march-1832/1.

call was subsequently transferred to Frederick G. Williams" (Doctrine and Covenants 81, section heading).

JESSE GAUSE

Jesse Gause, a schoolteacher, was born in 1784 in Pennsylvania and moved multiple times between, Delaware, Massachusetts, and Ohio. He became a member of the Society of Friends (Quakers) in 1806 and married his first wife, Martha Johnson, in 1815. She died in 1828, and he transferred his religious allegiance to the United Society of Believers in Christ's Second Appearing (Shakers) the following year. Despite the Shaker tenet that celibacy was a preferred lifestyle, he married Minerva Byram in 1830 and moved to the Shaker community at North Union, Ohio, in 1831 (see also Doctrine and Covenants 49). He was baptized early in 1832[6] and served as a scribe for the Bible translation in the Johnson Home in early March of that year. His call to serve as "a counselor unto my servant Joseph Smith, Jun." (D&C 81:1) as a new member occurred while he was serving as a scribe. The divine direction Joseph received may have had something to do with Jesse's knowledge of the Shakers' relative success in having "all things common" (Acts 4:32), knowledge that could have aided the Prophet in implementing the law of consecration.

The original manuscript of this revelation now known as section 81 is not extant but was probably written in Jesse's handwriting. Frederick G. Williams copied the revelation into the Kirtland Revelation Book soon thereafter and was appointed to replace him in January 1833. Oliver Cowdery replaced Jesse's name with Frederick's in the Kirtland Revelation Book, and Frederick's name appeared in subsequent publications of the revelations commencing with the first edition of the Doctrine and Covenants. The *Joseph Smith Papers* editors suggest "this indicates that (Joseph) and others regarded this revelation as containing general information about the duties of a counselor, rather than instructions specific to Gause."[7]

---

6. D. Michael Quinn, "Jesse Gause: Joseph Smith's Little-Known Counselor," Brigham Young University Studies, 23(4), 487–493.
7. "Revelation, 15 March 1832 [D&C 81]," josephsmithpapers.org/paper-summary/revelation-15-march-1832-dc-81/1#historical-intro.

Jesse was promised that if he was "faithful in counsel, in the office which I have appointed unto (him), . . . also in (the) ministry in proclaiming the gospel" (Doctrine and Covenants 81:3) he would have "a crown of immortality, and eternal life in the mansions which I have prepared in the house of my Father" (verse 6). He began serving a mission August 1 with Zebedee Coltrin to the Shaker community at North Union as well as to Thompson, Ohio, and Pittsburgh. He visited his wife in the Shaker community, apparently while on his mission, but was unsuccessful in convincing her to join him as a member of the Church. When Zebedee fell ill and was forced to return to Kirtland that same month, Jesse abandoned his mission and failed to continue as a counselor to the Prophet and was eventually excommunicated on 3 December 1832.[8]

SIDNEY RIGDON

Sidney Rigdon, Joseph's other counselor, also experienced personal difficulties at about the same time. Sidney's history suggests he suffered from mild bouts of depression from time to time, and that the head trauma he experienced on the night of the tar and feathering on 24 March 1832 affected his mental clarity. Following his second trip to Missouri, Sidney's weakened condition got the best of him in a meeting on 5 July 1832 in Kirtland. (Joseph and Emma had returned to Hiram.) Philo Dibble recorded what happened when Joseph Sr., who was conducting a prayer meeting, asked Sidney to preach, Sidney taught, "'The keys of kingdom are rent from the church nor would they be returned until the saints build him a new house.' On hearing this, many of his hearers wept, and when someone undertook to dismiss the meeting by prayer he said praying would do them no good, and the meeting broke up in confusion."[9]

Alarmed by what he heard, Hyrum Smith borrowed Philo's horse and carriage and drove all night to retrieve Joseph. Upon their return

8. Journal, 1832–1834, *The Joseph Smith Papers*, josephsmithpapers.org/paper-summary/journal-1832–1834/4.

9. Philo Dibble's Narrative, *Early Scenes in Church History: Four Faith Promoting Classics*, (Salt Lake City: Bookcraft, 1968), pp. 74–96.

to Kirtland, the Prophet "held a meeting in a large barn. Nearly all the inhabitants of Kirtland turned out to hear him. The barn was filled with people, and others, unable to get inside, stood around the door as far as they could hear. Joseph arose in our midst and spoke in mighty power, saying: 'I can contend with wicked men and devils— yes with angels. No power can pluck those keys from me, except the power that gave them to me; that was Peter, James and John. But for what Sidney [Rigdon] has done, the devil shall handle him as one man handles another.'"[10]

Sidney was released as Joseph's counselor, and Philo described the subsequent fulfillment of Joseph's prophecy: "About three weeks after this, Sidney was lying on his bed alone. An unseen power lifted him from his bed, threw him across the room, and tossed him from one side of the room to the other. The noise being heard in the adjoining room, his family went in to see what was the matter, and found him going from one side of the room to the other, from the effects of which Sidney was laid up for five or six weeks."[11]

Joseph explained the reasons for Sidney's behavior in a letter to W. W. Phelps:

> When Bro Sidney learned the feelings of the Brethren in whom he had placed so much confidence for whom he had endured so much fateague & suffering & whom he loved with so much love his heart was grieved his spirits failed & for a moment he became frantick & the advisary taking the advantage, he spake unadvisedly with his lips after receiving a severe chastisement resigned his commision and became a private member in the church, but has since repented like Peter of old and after a little suffering by the buffiting of Satan had been restored to his high standing in the church of God.[12]

---

10. Philo Dibble's Narrative, *Early Scenes in Church History: Four Faith Promoting Classics.*
11. Ibid.
12. Letter to William W. Phelps, 31 July 1832, The Joseph Smith Papers, joseph-smithpapers.org/paper-summary/letter-to-william-w-phelps-31–july-1832/1.

Joseph re-ordained Sidney as a counselor on 28 July, thus solving part of the difficulty associated with not having the support of formally called counselors. About five months later, the Lord revealed that his "Servent Frederick" was "called to be a Councillor & scribe unto my Servent Joseph."[13]

FREDERICK G. WILLIAMS

Frederick Granger Williams, eighteen years Joseph's senior, had been a doctor as well as a boat operator, farmer, and school teacher. He was one of the early Kirtland converts baptized in October 1830, and joined the four missionaries as they continued on to Missouri. He was serving as one of Joseph's scribes at the time he was called as a counselor to the Prophet in 1833. He also later served as paymaster of Zion's Camp, trustee of the School of the Prophets, justice of the peace in Kirtland, editor of several newspapers, and his experience and skills as a physician were held in high regard. When the Kirtland Safety Society collapsed in 1837, of which he was the president, he was one of the Church leaders who allowed themselves to be deceived into turning against the Prophet for which he was excommunicated in March 1839. His period of separation was relatively short, and he was received back into full fellowship a year later. His deep friendship with Joseph led to the Prophet and Emma naming their second surviving son after him. He suffered the mob persecutions of 1838 with the Missouri Saints and migrated to Illinois. He died from a lung hemorrhage in October 1842 in Quincy, Illinois.

On 8 March 1833, six months after Joseph and Emma moved back to Kirtland to live in the upstairs parlor of the Whitney Store, the Lord enhanced and formalized the roles that Sidney and Frederick held as Joseph's counselors by indicating they were "accounted as equal with thee in holding the keys of the last kingdom" (Doctrine and Covenants 90:6). Ten days later, following Sidney's request that he proceed with the revelation's directions, Joseph ordained Sidney and Frederick as his counselors, first and second respectively, and

---

13. Revelation, 5 January 1833, *The Joseph Smith Papers*, josephsmithpapers.org/paper-summary/revelation-5–january-1833/1.

conferred the keys in the School of the Prophets room in the Whitney Store. Thus, the process of creating an important component of church structure, the quorum of the First Presidency, was more or less complete. In a continuation of divine manifestations in Ohio that began on the Morley farm and continued in Hiram and in the Whitney Store, "many of the brethren saw a heavenly vision of the Savior, and concourses of angels, and many other things, of which each one has a record of what he saw.[14]

Three days later, Frederick received a license stating he had been "ordained to the Presidency of the High priesthood"[15] which represents a change in the usage of the term "presidency" as described previously. In February 1834, the Lord referred to the presidency of the high priesthood as "the First Presidency (D&C 102:26–27), all three members of the First Presidency as "presidents" (verse 3), the Prophet as "the president" and again all three members as "presidents" (verse 33). The use of the term "First Presidency" made it clear that its authority exceeded that of local presidents of the Church such as the "Presidency of the Church in Missouri," David Whitmer, W. W. Phelps, and John Whitmer, who were in effect a stake presidency of sorts similar to stake presidents today[16]

ADDITIONAL COUNSELORS

At times, additional counselors or assistant presidents were and are appointed to assist the First Presidency in managing the affairs of the Church. The first to be added was Oliver Cowdery. The Lord had appointed him second elder of the Church as it was first organized (see D&C 20:2–3; 21:11–12) in fulfillment of the instruction of John the Baptist (see JS—H 1:72). As Oliver's subsequent assignments took him to Missouri for significant periods of time, starting with his mission in October 1830, the Lord called Sidney

---

14. History of the Church, 1:334–35.
15. License for Frederick G. Williams, 20 Mar. 1833, The Joseph Smith Papers, josephsmithpapers.org/paper-summary/license-for-frederick-g-williams -20–march-1833/1.
16. Minutes and Discourse, circa 7 July 1834, The Joseph Smith Papers, josephsmith-papers.org/paper-summary/minutes-and-discourse-circa-7–july-1834/2).

Rigdon to assist the Prophet as his counselor. When Oliver returned to Kirtland in September 1833 as the Missouri persecutions were coming to a head, there was some confusion as to his role in the First Presidency and where he fit in the leadership hierarchy. This confusion was officially clarified on 5 December 1834, placing him in a position of authority above Sidney[17] as an assistant president, or associate president, second only to Joseph. In fact, if Joseph would have died during the time Oliver occupied this position, Oliver would have become President of the Church. Hyrum Smith was in the same position when he was called to replace Oliver after Oliver left the Church. (A more complete discussion of the keys held by Joseph, Oliver, and Hyrum appears in the appendix.) The following day Hyrum and Joseph Smith Sr. were also ordained as additional assistants or counselors in the First Presidency.[18]

17. Journal, 1834–1836, The Joseph Smith Papers, josephsmithpapers.org/paper-summary/journal-1832–1834/94#historical-intro.

18. History, 1834–1836, *The Joseph Smith Papers*, josephsmithpapers.org/paper-summary/history-1834–1836/22). The Prophet's uncle, John Smith, was added to the First Presidency in 1837 ("Minute Book 1," Joseph Smith Papers, josephsmithpapers.org/paper-summary/minute-book-1/238).

CHRONOLOGICAL SUMMARY

Summer 1832:   First Vision account

Mid/late June: Return from Missouri to Kirtland

~1 July 1832:   Return to Johnson Home

5 July 1832:   Sidney Rigdon preaches, keys taken from the Church

7 July 1832:   Sidney released as counselor

23 July 1832:   Sidney re-ordained as counselor

29 Aug. 1832:   Revelation for John Murdock (section 99)

12 Sept. 1832:   Joseph, Emma, and family move back to Kirtland

Dec. 1832:   Jesse Gause released as first counselor

18 Mar. 1833:   Sidney Rigdon and Frederick G. Williams ordained

Chapter 13

Concluding a Marvelous Year of Revelation

O n 1 April 1832, a week after Joseph Smith and Sidney Rigdon had been tarred and feathered, they joined Newell K. Whitney, Jesse Gause, and Peter Whitmer, Jr in traveling to Missouri to establish the United Firm in response to the Lord's direction given on 1 March (see Doctrine & Covenants 78:9) They arrived on 24 March. (Joseph had sent Emma and daughter Julia to Kirtland to stay with Ann Whitney to ensure their safety. Unknown to Joseph, Ann's Aunt Sarah objected to having them stay, and Emma and Julia were forced to find housing with Emma's in-laws, the Williams, and the Cahoons. Joseph found her "very disconsolate"[1] on his return.

INTERRUPTED JOURNEY

After twelve days in Missouri, Joseph, Sidney, and Newell left for Kirtland on 6 May. While they were traveling through Indiana, the horses pulling their stage became frightened, placing the brethren in danger. Newell attempted to jump from the stage, but his coat caught

---

1. History, 1838–1856, volume A-1 [23 December 1805–30 August 1834], The Joseph Smith Papers. josephsmithpapers.org/paper-summary/history-1838–1856–volume-a-1–23–december-1805–30–august-1834/215.

in the door, causing his foot to catch in a stage wheel and breaking his leg in several places. Sidney proceeded on while Joseph remained with Newell in Greenville, in a "public house"[2] where Joseph tended to him for another month. Newell was well treated by the tavern owner, but Joseph was not. While Newell was convalescing, Joseph frequently took morning walks. On one such walk Joseph felt violent stomach convulsions that caused him to vomit poisoned food along with large quantities of blood, severely dislocating his jaw. He adjusted his jaw himself and managed to make his way to the tavern. He wrote, "[Newell] administered to me in the name of the Lord, and I was healed in an instant, although the effect of the poison was so powerful, as to cause much of the hair to become loosened from my head. Thanks be to my Heavenly Father for His interference in my behalf at this critical moment, in the name of Jesus Christ. Amen."[3]

On 2 June they received a visit from Martin Harris, who brought news that their families were well. On 6 June Joseph wrote to Emma, suggesting that he and Newell would soon be traveling home and that remaining in Indiana had been anything but pleasant. "My Situation is a very unpleasent one although I will endeaver to be Contented the Lord asisting me I have visited a grove which is Just back of the town almost every day where I can be Secluded from the eyes of any mortal and there give vent to all the feelings of my heart in meaditation and prayr."[4]

Shortly after Martin's visit, Joseph made a suggestion to Newell regarding their return to Kirtland that demonstrates his seership:

> If he would agree to start for home in the morning, we would take a wagon to the river, about four miles, and there would be a ferry-boat

2. History, 1838–1856, volume A-1 [23 December 1805–30 August 1834], p. 214, The Joseph Smith Papers, accessed 3 May 2019. josephsmith papers.org/paper-summary/history-1838–1856–volume-a-1–23–december-1805–30–august-1834/215.

3. History, 1838–1856, volume A-1 [23 December 1805–30 August 1834], The Joseph Smith Papers. josephsmithpapers.org/paper-summary/history-1838–1856–volume-a-1–23–december-1805–30–august-1834/221

4. Joseph Smith, "Chapter 20: A Heart Full of Love and Faith: The Prophet's Letters to His Family," Teachings of Presidents of the Church: Joseph Smith, (2011). lds.org/manual/teachings-joseph-smith-chapter-20?lang=eng

in waiting which would take us quickly across, where we would find a hack which would take us directly to the landing, where we should find a boat, in waiting, and we would be going up the river before ten o'clock, and have a prosperous journey home. He took courage and told me he would go. We started next morning, and found everything as I had told him, for we were passing rapidly up the river before ten o'clock, and, landing at Wellsville, took stage coach to Chardon, from thence in a wagon to Kirtland.[5]

AMASA LYMAN

Joseph remained in Kirtland with Emma and Julia for a few days and returned to the Johnsons' home around 1 July. There he was met by a new young convert named Amasa Lyman, who had been baptized by Lyman Johnson in April, spent a brief time in Palmyra, arrived in Hiram about a month before Joseph's arrival, and was employed as a hired hand. He recounts the spiritual experience he had in first meeting the Prophet. "When he grasped my hand in the cordial way (known to those who have met him in the honest simplicity of truth,) I felt as one of old in the presence of the Lord, my strength seemed to be gone, so that it required an effort on my part to stand on my feet; but in all this there was no fear, but the serenity and peace of heaven pervaded my soul, and the still small voice of the spirit whispered its living testimony in the depths of my soul, where it has ever remained, that he was a Man of God."[6]

Amasa became an important figure in Church leadership. He traveled with Zion's Camp and was among the first brethren to be ordained a Seventy. He remained faithful at the collapse of the Kirtland Safety Society in which he held stock. He was ordained an Apostle in 1842 and served in the First Presidency from 1843 to 1844. He led wagon companies to the Salt Lake Valley, served a mission to South Dakota to reclaim the Saints who were following the apostate James Emmett,

---

5. History, 1838–1856, volume A-1 [23 December 1805–30 August 1834], *The Joseph Smith Papers*. josephsmithpapers.org/paper-summary/history-1838 –1856–volume-a-1–23–december-1805–30–august-1834/215.

6. Amasa Mason Lyman, "Amasa Lyman's History," *Deseret News*, (September 8, 1858, 1).

established a settlement in San Bernardino, California, and then went on to preside over the European Mission from 1860 to 1862. Ironically, he was dropped from the Quorum of the Twelve for teaching false doctrine in 1876 and was excommunicated in 1880. He took leadership of the Godbeite Church of Zion that same year and eventually died in Fillmore, Utah. Although one of his wives and some of his children followed him into apostasy, others remained faithful, and three of his descendants eventually served as Apostles—Francis Lyman, Richard R. Lyman, and James E. Faust, who later served in the First Presidency.

After Joseph arranged his "affairs," he "recommenced the translation of the Scriptures and thus "spent most of [the]summer,"[7] receiving scribal assistance from Frederick G. Williams, a precursor to Frederick receiving the call to replace Jesse Gause as a counselor to the Prophet. This modest description of his endeavors for the remainder of the summer only lightly touch upon his experiences, which proved to be of great importance to him and the restoration.

THE FIRST EDITION OF THE EVENING AND MORNING STAR

In July the Prophet noted in his history that he received the first edition of *The Evening and Morning Star* from Independence. This endeavor marked the beginning of a long, continuous printing effort by the Church that has included scriptures, books, periodicals, hymnals, and newspapers—the *Star*, the *Messenger and Advocate* in Kirtland, the *Elders' Journal* in Far West, the *Times and Seasons* in Nauvoo, the *Millennial Star* in Britain, and the *Deseret News* in Salt Lake City, among others. Referring to it as "a joyous treat," Joseph wrote, "Delightful, indeed, was it to contemplate that the little band of brethren had become so large, and grown so strong, in so short a time as to be able to issue a paper of their own, which contained not only some of the revelations, but other information also—which

---

7.   History, 1838–1856, volume A-1 [23 December 1805–30 August 1834], *The Joseph Smith Papers*.

would gratify and enlighten the humbler inquirer after truth."[8] Joseph's delight was amplified when he compared this milestone to the treatment the Church had received from the press that had been "universally arrayed against us."[9] Joseph characterized the benefit such literature provides: "Editors thought to do us harm, while the Saints rejoiced that they could do nothing against the truth but for it."[10]

TROUBLES WITH JOSEPH'S COUNSELORS

Although the notion of a First Presidency was still evolving, the Lord had directed Joseph to select Sidney Rigdon and Jesse Gause as counselors in March 1832. In early July, Sidney's occasional mental difficulties got the best of him, and he preached in Kirtland that the "keys of the kingdom are rent from the church,"[11] which caused a great stir. Joseph traveled to Kirtland from Hiram and preached to a crowd in a local barn filled to overflowing where he said, "No power can pluck those keys from me, . . . But for what Sidney [Rigdon] has done, the devil shall handle him as one man handles another."[12] Joseph's efforts quelled the storm, and Sidney was released from his position. A few weeks later Sidney did indeed suffer from an evil influence, and Joseph returned a repentant Sidney to his position.

Jesse Gause was a relatively recent convert who had served briefly as Joseph's scribe and had received divine direction that accompanied his call to serve as a counselor (see Doctrine and Covenants 81). He was born in 1784 and joined the Society of Friends (Quakers) in 1806. By August 1829 he had joined the United Society of Believers in Christ's Second Appearing (Shakers). He moved with his second wife, Minerva, to the Shaker community at North Union, Cuyahoga County, Ohio, sometime in 1831 and around that time was baptized, possibly by Reynolds Cahoon, but his wife did not join with him.[13] He

---

8.   Ibid.
9.   Ibid.
10. Ibid.
11. Philo Dibble, "Philo Dibble, 1806–1895. Autobiography (1806–c. 1843)", boap.org/LDS/Early-Saints/PDibble.html.
12. Philo Dibble, "Philo Dibble, 1806–1895. Autobiography (1806–c. 1843)."
13. Robert J. Woodford, "Jesse Gause, Counselor to the Prophet," *BYU Studies*, 3

traveled to Missouri with the Prophet in April 1832 and was appointed a member of the United Firm. He returned to Kirtland in June, then left for a mission on 1 August 1832 with Zebedee Coltrin. He traveled to the Shaker community in a vain effort to Minerva. When Zebedee had to return to Kirtland because of illness, Jesse left his mission and was not heard from again. Joseph removed him from his position as counselor in December, after moving back to Kirtland, and the Lord revealed that Frederick G. Williams should take Jesse's place.

THE PROPHET'S 1832 HISTORY

One of the more recent treasures discovered amidst the records of the Church is Joseph's 1832 history written in his own and Frederick G. Williams' handwriting. Although somewhat rough and unpolished, it sheds light on the Prophet's other recorded histories relating to his early prophetic experiences. It represents the first extant recording of some of the early events in the Restoration and was most likely written between 20 July and 22 September 1832, probably in the Johnsons' home. It begins: "A History of the life of Joseph Smith Jr. an account of his marvilous experience and of all the mighty acts which he doeth in the name of Jesus Ch[r]ist . . . and also an account of the rise of the church of Christ in the eve of time."[14]

The Prophet's written intent stated in the beginning of the history was to describe the events leading up to and including "the testimony from on high" (the First Vision), "the ministering of Angels" (the visitation of Moroni and the coming forth of the Book of Mormon), the "reception of the holy Priesthood" (the conferral of the Aaronic Priesthood by John the Baptist), and "a confirmation and reception of the high Priesthood (the conferral of the Melchizedek Priesthood by Peter, James, and John)."[15] For some unknown reason, the latter two events were never addressed in this history, but the First Vision is treated thoroughly, and the coming forth of the Book of Mormon is discussed up until the time of Oliver Cowdery's

---

no. 1, 1975, 362–364.

14. History, circa Summer 1832," The Joseph Smith Papers. josephsmithpapers. org/paper-summary/history-circa-summer-1832/2

15. History, circa Summer 1832," The Joseph Smith Papers.

arrival in Harmony, Pennsylvania. Its treatment of the First Vision has attracted the most recent attention, and when studied in combination with his three other accounts provides a harmonious and more comprehensive understanding. Those three other accounts were (a) a telling to Robert Matthews, the self-proclaimed "Prophet Matthias," recorded by Warren Parrish in 1835; (b) his official, later canonized, account that is part of his history begun in 1838, which is found in the Pearl of Great Price and first published in 1842; and (c) an 1842 account recorded in what has become known as the "Wentworth Letter," also published in 1842 but before the Pearl of Great Price version.

THE BAPTISM OF GEORGE ALBERT SMITH

Two days before his removal to Kirtland, Joseph's cousin George A. Smith was baptized. George was the son of the brother of Joseph Smith Sr., John Smith, and the grandfather of President George Albert Smith. John became a counselor in the First Presidency, and his son, George, eventually became an Apostle and counselor to Brigham Young. Joseph was very much concerned about his extended family's response to the Restoration, so receiving the news would have been especially gratifying, as anyone would feel as their efforts in sharing the gospel with their family bore fruit.

THE PROPHET AND EMMA LEAVE HIRAM

The tarring and feathering and Joseph's temporary absence from Hiram did not quell the public animosity toward him and the other Saints in the Hiram area, particularly among apostate members. By the time Joseph and Emma returned to Hiram in July, most of the Saints had moved to Kirtland, including Sidney Rigdon and his family, or to Missouri, and the Johnsons' home was no longer a tranquil place to continue the Bible translation. The mobs "continued to molest and menace father Johnson's house for a long time."[16] Joseph, Emma (who

---

16. "History, 1838–1856, volume A-1 [23 December 1805–30 August 1834]," 209, *The Joseph Smith Papers*. josephsmithpapers.org/paper-summary/history-1838–1856–volume-a-1–23–december-1805–30–august-1834/215)

was seven months pregnant), and baby Julia, now seventeen months old, left Hiram exactly one year later to the day they had arrived, on 12 September 1832, and would never return to the Johnson's home. Newell K. and Elizabeth Ann Whitney had been preparing an apartment for the Smiths on the second floor of their store. Although not finished until November, it was sufficiently complete to allow them to move in. It provided a place where the Bible translation was completed, and where the Lord continued to unfold His designs for this dispensation. The move of the Smith family to Kirtland, however, did not end the important role of the Johnsons and their Hiram home in the Restoration.

Continued Influence of the Johnson Family and the Johnson Home

LIVES OF THE JOHNSON FAMILY AFTER 1832

John Johnson Sr.

After the Prophet, Emma, and Julia left Hiram in September 1832, most of the faithful Saints moved to Missouri or Kirtland, while a few remained behind. Unfortunately, there also remained some former Saints who chose to leave the Church. John and Alice (Elsa) Johnson remained faithful but chose to leave Hiram a year later. They turned the operation of the farm over to their son Luke in the summer of 1833, then sold the farm to Jude and Patty Stevens when Luke moved to Kirtland. After having been one of the wealthiest families in Portage County with one of the most successful farms in the area,[1] John and Elsa became "land-rich but cash-poor." They were included on Kirtland's poor list and accordingly received

---

1. Mark Lyman Staker, *Hearken O Ye People: The Historical Setting of Joseph Smith's Ohio Revelations* (Salt Lake City, UT: Greg Kofford Books, 2009).

an "invitation" to leave the township. Their temporary poverty was due to the lengthy time required to complete the sale of their farm.

In Kirtland, John was ordained a high priest and served on the Kirtland Stake High Council. He was also called to participate in the United Firm (see Doctrine and Covenants 96:6–9), a Church business management entity of sorts that required its members to consecrate their assets and receive one of the consecrated properties and/or businesses as a stewardship. Stewardships would provide income for members and for the Church and resources for the bishop's storehouse. When the sale of their farm was finalized in May 1834 for $3,000 cash plus the Jude Stevens' farm a mile southwest of the temple in Kirtland, most of the proceeds were consecrated to the Church at a time when its debts could not be paid. The cash was used to finance the Zion's Camp march and part of the Peter French farm purchase where the temple and printing building were eventually built; Martin Harris was to receive the Stevens' farm (see Doctrine and Covenants 104:24). The members of the firm had decided to dissolve it on 10 April 1834, but two weeks later the Lord directed the firm to be reorganized and that "its properties were to be divided among members of the firm as their stewardships" (Doctrine and Covenants 104, section heading). John received much of the French farm property, excepting a few lots designated for the temple and for Oliver Cowdery. He managed the inn located on the property, which at that point housed a store and was the temporary location of the Church printing press. He sold a great deal of the property and eventually turned the inn back into a tavern, a motel of sorts, and it became known as the Johnson Inn. He later sold it to John Jr.

In a matter of a few years, John and Elsa Johnson had given nearly everything they had to the Church. They provided a home for the Prophet, his family, and his scribes. They housed and fed numerous missionaries and visitors, and they sold their farm and donated many of the proceeds to the Church. In addition, they sent their sons, who would have otherwise helped their father run the farm, on several missions. Father Johnson worked to sell Church properties and to fulfill his duties as a member of the high council. He also made donations to the building fund for the Kirtland Temple. In a blessing John received in April 1836, the Prophet said, "As thou hast been liberal with thy property as befit the saints thou shalt have an hundred fold in the stead thereof . . . and all that thy heart desires in righteousness before the Lord."[2]

Unfortunately, John was caught up in the fallout from the collapse of the Kirtland Safety Society in 1837 and was among the many prominent leaders whose ties to the Church were severed in one way or another. He was released from the Kirtland High Council and thereafter distanced himself from the Church, although he was not excommunicated. There is no record in which John explained this dramatic change, but it is likely these financial troubles contributed to his weakened commitment. He remained in Kirtland, where he passed away in 1843.

Alice (Elsa) Jacob Johnson

Very little is known of Elsa's activities in Kirtland following the Johnsons' move there, although she likely supported her husband in his service and generosity to the Church. Later she accompanied her husband in leaving the Church, but whether her decision was an indication of her feelings about the Church or simply a show of support for John is unclear. When John Sr. died, John, Jr. cared for Elsa, and she accompanied him to Council Bluffs, Iowa, in 1855. John Jr. moved there for business reasons, and there is no record of Elsa involving herself with the Church despite living in a place of importance in the Latter-day Saint migration to Utah. She died in 1870 at the age of eighty-nine.

Alice (Elsa) Johnson Olney

Alice, the Johnsons' firstborn child and oldest daughter, married Oliver Olney in 1820. Olney owned a farm and a textile business in the town of Mantua, near her parents in Portage County, Ohio. They moved their business to nearby Shalersville, also in Portage County, where they joined the Church and housed the first meetings of the Shalersville Branch in their home. They later moved to Kirtland,

---

2. John Johnson blessings, 1836, MS 2524, Church History Library, accessed 13 October 2018, dcms.lds.org/delivery/DeliveryManagerServlet ?dps_pid=IE12295003.

Missouri, and Nauvoo. Alice died in 1841, leaving behind seven children who were taken in by her sisters Fanny and Emily. Oliver was away from Nauvoo at the time of her death, and his involvement in either the lives of his children or the Church is uncertain.

Fanny Johnson Ryder

Fanny married Simonds Ryder's younger brother, Jason, in 1822, and lived on a farm bordering her father's and brother-in-law's properties in Hiram. The couple may or may not have joined the Church, but like Simonds, Jason was an active member of the Hiram congregation of the Disciples of Christ, as was Fanny. Fanny and Jason had eight children and raised one of Elsa Olney's children. Fanny remained in Hiram and died in 1879. Many of her descendants still live in the Hiram area.

John Johnson Jr.

John Jr. joined the Church around the time of his parents' conversion but left it a year later. He did, however, remain friendly with the Church thereafter. He owned a farm in Hiram and later moved with his parents to Kirtland, where he eventually purchased the Johnson Inn from his father. He moved his family and his mother to Council Bluffs, Iowa, in 1855, where he became a successful farmer. He married Eliza Ann Marcy in 1830. Although they had no children, they raised three of Elsa's. He died in 1887.

Olmstead G. Johnson

Olmstead was away from home at the time of his family's conversion and met the Prophet when he came home for a visit. Joseph told him that "if he did not obey the Gospel, the spirit he was of would lead him to destruction, and when he went away, he would never return or see his father again."[3] He ignored the warning and joined with the promoters of settlements in northern

---

3. History, 1838–1856, volume A-1 [23 December 1805–30 August 1834], The Joseph Smith Papers. josephsmithpapers.org/paper-summary/history-1838–1856–volume-a-1–23–december-1805–30–august-1834/198#full-transcript

Mexico. He ended up in Virginia, where he died in 1834 at the age of twenty-four.

Emily Hannah Johnson Quinn

Emily moved to Kirtland with her parents, where she later married Christopher Quinn Jr., a non-Latter-day Saint Irish immigrant, in 1837. Emily maintained her commitment to the Church but remained in Ohio when the Saints moved to Missouri. She had three children and raised one of her sister Elsa's daughters. She died in 1855 in Painesville, Ohio, at the age of forty-one, the same year her brother, John, gave up the Johnson Inn to Christopher when he left Kirtland for Council Bluffs.

Marinda Nancy Johnson Hyde

The family stayed with Orson when he was assigned to remain behind in Kanesville, Iowa, when the rest of the Quorum of the Twelve continued west, presiding over the Saints who made temporary homes in Iowa until 1852, when they moved to Salt Lake City. Orson again left his family to begin a settlement in Carson Valley, Nevada, and presided over the Saints in Sanpete County, Utah, where he also established households for his plural wives. Marinda remained in Salt Lake running a boarding house to provide income for her family and divorced Orson in 1870. Marinda maintained her connection with the Ohio members of her family, traveling there in 1876, and remained faithful to the Church. She died ten years later at the age of seventy-one.

Mary Beal Johnson

Mary was fifteen when her family moved to Kirtland in 1833. Shortly after, she served as a live-in caregiver to Joseph and Emma's children in their apartment in the Whitney Store. That same year she fell ill and died, "which caused much gloominess at the prophet's house."[4]

---

4. Pamela Call Johnson, *Joseph Holbrook: Mormon Pioneer, a Journal* (Bloomington, IN: Author House: 2013, 25).

Justin Jacob Johnson

Justin was twelve when his parents left Hiram. He moved to Nauvoo at some point, which suggests that he stayed committed to the Church after his parents' inactivity. He worked as a school teacher there and married Mary Ann Ivins in 1846 in Fort Madison, Iowa. His first two children were born after he and Mary Ann moved back to Kirtland, and by 1860 Justin had settled close to John Jr. and his mother, in the vicinity of Council Bluffs, Iowa, where he farmed. He remained in Iowa until his death in 1894 at the age of seventy-four.

THE HOME

For many years the Stevens family, having purchased the Johnsons' home, regularly welcomed visitors who wanted to see where the "Mormon Prophet" had lived. They kept a scrapbook of old local newspaper clippings concerning the home's history, which they shared with the visitors, and invited them upstairs to the room they referred to as the "translation room," where they told stories about the Johnson family and the events that occurred in their home.

Ownership

The farm remained in the Stevens family until the Church purchased it in 1956 from the Monroes, relatives of the Stevens, who were also descendants of Jason and Fanny Johnson Ryder. Over the years the home underwent numerous remodelings, including a layer of wood shakes and another of aluminum siding covering the original clapboard exterior. Several layers of paint were added to the interior, and wall configurations were adjusted. The stoop and a well on the west side were covered up, and bricks from an original fireplace were used to create a tunnel for air heated by a furnace under the carriage house. Underneath it all, much of the original home structure remained intact.

The Johnson farm was the first former Church history site in Ohio purchased by the Church. The story of its acquisition in 1956 by Wilford Wood, a member of the Church Historic Sites Committee, is miraculous. In a letter to President McKay, Wilford related that after a day of negotiations with the Monroe family, during which it seemed he wasn't making much progress, he was invited to spend the night in the "revelation room." He was awakened in the middle of the night by a visit from the Prophet Joseph Smith, who was standing next to his bed. Joseph gave him explicit instructions about what to say and what language should be included in the contract, assuring Wilford the Monroes would approve it. Wilford stated that Joseph smiled throughout his visit; he characterized it as "sublime." Although the sale price listed in the contract was far below the Monroes' offer, they signed it the next day, just as Joseph had promised.[5]

Wilford reported that Joseph had also shown him where the tarring and feathering had taken place, a thousand-foot-square parcel just south and west of the Johnson Home. Joseph asked that it be memorialized in some fashion, so Wilford planted a border of trees around it.[6] Subsequent land transactions resulted in the parcel returning to local ownership. All together, Wilford Wood was responsible for acquiring ten historic sites and/or buildings in various locations as well as several historical documents.

Transformation to Historic Site

After acquisition by the Church, the former Johnson property sat dormant for a time. Later under the direction of local Church authorities, the property became a welfare farm, and the home was used as a residence for the farm manager, Junior Stalnaker, and his family, as well as the Hiram Branch meetinghouse. In 1969 the home was dedicated by Elder Mark E. Petersen as a historic site, and missionaries were assigned to give tours and live in the home in its somewhat remodeled condition along with the family. Exhibits were set up telling of the standard works of the Church and the doctrines contained in section 76. The process of returning the home to its original

---

5. J. B. Haws, "Wilford Wood's Twentieth-Century Treks East: A Visionary's Mission to Preserve Historic Sites," in *Far Away in the West: Reflections on the Mormon Pioneer Trail*, ed. Scott C. Esplin, Richard E. Bennett, Susan Easton Black, and Craig K. Manscill (Provo, UT: Religious Studies Center).

6. Ibid.

appearance began with a number of minor restorations with a project in the 1980s.

In 1996, President Gordon B. Hinckley directed that the transformation to the home's 1831–32 appearance be completed. This restoration required five years, which included extensive research into the Johnson family, their home, and the times in which they lived. During the dedicatory service on 28 October 2001, President Gordon B. Hinckley prayed, "We dedicate and consecrate the John Johnson home as a place sacred unto Thee and unto us, as a place in which Thou didst reveal Thyself with Thy Beloved Son."[7]

The house has been restored as close as possible to the look and feel of the home when Joseph Smith lived there in 1831–32. Since its dedication, thousands of people have toured the Johnson Home and experienced a powerful outpouring of the Spirit testifying of the reality of the resurrected Savior of the world, His restored gospel, and His Prophet, Joseph Smith. That same power, President Hinckley promised, "that was expressed in that farmhouse . . . has gone over the earth . . . and we have scarcely seen the beginning of it. So long as this Church lasts, . . . so long as its history is written and known, the John Johnson home will have a prominent place in that history."[8]

---

7. Shaun D. Stahle, "John Johnson Home Will have a Place in History," *Church News* (3 November 2001), 3.
8. Shaun D. Stahle, "John Johnson Home Will have a Place in History."

Appendix A

Kirtland Chronology

© 2015 Damon L. Bahr
*occurred elsewhere

Key Events Arranged Chronologically	D&C Sections-LDS	Places	Year
To Ohio, Establish prophetic leadership, 1st Bishop, The Law	41-44	Whitney Home	
JST (on-going) Elsa Johnson healing (NKW home), Spiritual gifts	45-50, 51*, 52-56, 57-62*, 63-64	Morley Farm	1831
NY Saints, 1st High Priests, Vision of Father & Son, Son presence			
Missouri - Zion revealed, Land dedicated, Temple cornerstones			
JST (on-going), Conference at Orange	66, 65, 1, 68, 67, 133, 69, 107 pt, 70, 72*, 71, 73, 75*, 132?, 76, 77, 78*, 79-81, 82-83*, 99	Johnson Home	1832
Book of Commandments, Preaching to undo Ezra Boothe articles			
President of High Priesthood, Vision of Father & Son (D&C 76)			
Counselors to President of High Priesthood, Tar & Feathering			
Missouri - Printing & contention			
Difficulties with counselors to President of High Priesthood			
JST (on-going), Joseph Smith with Whitney to Albany, Boston, & NYC	84-93, 95-96, 94, 97-98, 100*, 101	Whitney Store	1833
Frederick G. Williams in First Presidency, Joseph Smith III born			
Temple land search & purchase, School of the Prophets			
First Presidency fully organized, Appearance of Father and Son			
Temple cornerstone ceremony & construction			
Missouri - Persecutions & press destroyed			
Joseph Smith travels with Freeman Nickerson to Canada			
First Patriarchal Blessings and Vision of the Son (Johnson Inn)			
Kirtland Stake & High Council	102-104, 105*, 106, 107 pt.*, 134*, 108, 137*, 109-110*, 111*, 112*	Joseph & Emma Smith Home	1834
Prophecy - Rocky Mtns. & Church filling the world (Morley Farm)			
Zion's Camp march to redeem Zion			
Missouri Presidency & High Council			
Temple Construction, JS Travels to Michigan, School of Prophets			1835
Lectures on Faith, Printing Office by Temple			
Quorum of the Twelve, Multiple quorums of Seventies			
Doctrine & Covenants prepared			
Mission of the Twelve to the east			
Mummies, Book of Abraham commenced, D&C printed & approved			
Hebrew study commenced, Travel to Michigan			
Priesthood quorums organized			
Temple ordinances, 3 or 4 visions of Father & Son, 2 visions of the Son			1836
2 Dedications, Solemn Assembly, 2 visions of Son, Keys, Priesthood mtg.			
Temple ordinances continue for others			
Joseph Smith travels to New York, Massachusetts			
Fast and Testimony meetings commenced by this time			
Twelve return from missions - observe prosperity, greed, speculation			1837
Kirtland Safety Society opens			
2nd edition Book of Mormon published, JS Travels to Michigan			
Twelve leave on mission to England			
Joseph Smith resigns from Kirtland Safety Society			
3 Apostles disciplined, Missouri - changes in 1st Presidency			
Kirtland Safety Society closes			

Appendix B
All the Keys

The conferral of all priesthood keys that have been restored in this dispensation to others besides Joseph Smith during the Prophet's lifetime is well documented. Joseph Fielding Smith taught about their bestowal upon Oliver Cowdery and Hyrum Smith.

On 5 December 1834 the Prophet Joseph Smith ordained Oliver Cowdery as Assistant President of the Church [see History of the Church, 2:176]. He had been with the Prophet when the Aaronic and Melchizedek Priesthoods were restored. When the Church of Jesus Christ was organized in 1830, Oliver as "second elder" stood next to Joseph in authority [see D&C 20:2–3]. Thus, whenever priesthood authority or keys were restored, Oliver was with the Prophet Joseph. It was necessary, according to the divine law of witnesses, for Joseph Smith to have a companion holding those keys.

The Lord called Oliver Cowdery as the second witness to stand at the head of this dispensation assisting the Prophet in holding the keys. The records inform us that every time the Prophet received authority and the keys of the priesthood from the heavens, Oliver Cowdery shared in the conferring of those powers with the Prophet. Had Oliver Cowdery remained faithful and had he survived the Prophet under those conditions, he would have succeeded as President of the Church by virtue of this divine calling.

On January 19, 1841, because Oliver did not remain faithful, "the Lord commanded Joseph Smith to ordain Hyrum Smith and confer upon him all the keys, authority, and privileges placed upon the head of Oliver Cowdery, and make him the 'Second President' of the Church."[1]

Brigham Young also taught regarding the conferral of keys upon Hyrum Smith: "If Hyrum had lived he would not have stood between Joseph and the Twelve but he would have stood for Joseph.—Did Joseph ordain any man to take his place? He did. Who was it? It was Hyrum, but, Hyrum fell a martyr before Joseph did. If Hyrum had lived he would have acted for Joseph."[2]

Wilford Woodruff spoke of the conferral of keys upon the Twelve.

> I am a living witness to the testimony that [Joseph Smith] gave to the Twelve Apostles when all of us received our endowments from under his hands. I remember the last speech that he ever gave us before his death. It was before we started upon our mission to the East. He stood upon his feet some three hours. The room was filled as with consuming fire, his face was as clear as amber, and he was clothed upon by the power of God. He laid before us our duty. He laid before us the fullness of this great work of God; and in his remarks to us he said: 'I have had sealed upon my head every key, every power, every principle of life and salvation that God has ever given to any man who ever lived upon the face of the earth. And these principles and this Priesthood and power belong to this great and last dispensation which the God of Heaven has set His hand to establish in the earth. "Now," said he addressing the Twelve, "I have sealed upon your heads every key, every power, and every principle which the Lord has sealed upon my head." . . .
>
> After addressing us in this manner he said: "I tell you, the burden of this kingdom now rests upon your shoulders; you have got to bear it off in all the world."[3]

1. Joseph Fielding Smith, *Doctrines of Salvation*, Bruce R. McConkie, ed.,1:211, 213, 220.
2. "Conference Minutes," *Times and Seasons*, Oct. 15, 1844, 683.
3. *Teachings of Presidents of the Church: Wilford Woodruff.* (Salt Lake City, UT: The Church of Jesus Christ of Latter-day Saints, 2004), xxxii.

President Joseph Fielding Smith explained why we no longer have an Assistant President in the Church.

> The question is sometimes asked: If Oliver Cowdery was ordained to hold the keys jointly with the Prophet, and after his loss by transgression, this authority was conferred on Hyrum Smith, then why do we not have today in the Church the same order of things, and an Assistant President as well as two counselors in the First Presidency?
>
> The answer to this is a simple one. It is because the peculiar condition requiring two witnesses to establish the work, is not required after the work is established. Joseph and Hyrum Smith stand at the head of this dispensation, jointly holding the keys, as the two necessary witnesses fulfilling the law as it is set down by our Lord in his answer to the Jews [see Matthew 18:16]. Since the gospel will never again be restored there will be no occasion for this condition to arise again. We all look back to the two special witnesses, called to bear witness in full accord with the divine law.[4]

---

4. Joseph Field Smith, *Church History in the Fulness of Times*, 2nd ed. (Salt Lake City, UT: The Church of Jesus Christ of Latter-day Saints, 2004), 153.

Appendix C
Apostleship

We will now commence with the Apostleship where Joseph commenced. Joseph was ordained an Apostle—that you can read and understand. After he was ordained to this office, he had the right to organize and build up the kingdom of God, for he had committed unto him the keys of the priesthood, which is after the order of Melchizedek—the High Priesthood, which is after the order of the Son of God. And this, remember, by being ordained an Apostle. Could he have built up the Kingdom of God, without first being an Apostle? No, he never could. The keys of the eternal priesthood, which is after the order of the Son of God, are comprehended by being an Apostle. All the priesthood, all the keys, all the gifts, all the endowments, and everything preparatory to entering into the presence of the Father and of the Son, are in, composed of, circumscribed by, or I might say incorporated within the circumference of the Apostleship.[1]

---

1. Eldon J. Watson, (ed). *Brigham Young Addresses, a Chronological Compilation of Known Addresses of the Prophet Brigham Young,* (Salt Lake City, Utah: Eldon Jay Watson, 1968), 2(06).

Appendix D

Ordination of the Twelve Apostles

Date/ Location	Who was ordained (and by whom)	Reference
Feb 14/ Schoolhouse (Printing Office)	Lyman Johnson Brigham Young Heber C. Kimball (3 witnesses)	*Richard E. Turley, "23. The Calling of the Twelve Apostles and the Seventy in 1835," BYU Religious Studies Center, accessed 26 November 2018, rsc.byu.edu/archived/joseph-smith-and-doctrinal-restoration/23–calling-twelve-apostles-and-seventy-1835 *Minutes, Discourse, and Blessings, 14–15 February 1835, 149. The Joseph Smith Papers, accessed 26 November 2018, josephsmithpapers.org/paper-summary/minutes-discourse-and-blessings-14–15–february-1835/3

Feb 15/ Schoolhouse (Printing Office)	Orson Hyde David W. Patten Luke Johnson William E. McLellin John F. Boynton William Smith (3 witnesses: Oliver Cowdery [voice] and Joseph Smith additional participant for Orson, David, Luke at least)	*Minutes, Discourse, and Blessings, 14–15 February 1835, 151. *The Joseph Smith Papers*, accessed 26 November 2018, josephsmithpapers.org/paper-summary/minutes-discourse-and-blessings-14–15–february-1835/3
Feb 21/ Schoolhouse (Printing Office)	Parley P. Pratt[3, 5] (Joseph Smith[3, 5] Oliver Cowdery[3, 5] [voice] David Whitmer)[3, 5]	*Parley Parker Pratt, *The Autobiography of Parley Parker Pratt*, ed. Parley P. Pratt (Chicago: Law, King & Law, 1874), 127. *Minute Book* (Minutes and Blessings, 21 February 1835)
Apr 26/ Temple[4] (unfinished)	Thomas B. Marsh[4] Orson Pratt[4] (Oliver Cowdery[4] [voice], David Whitmer)[4]	*Minute Book* (Minutes 26 April 1835). *Richard E. Turley, "23. The Calling of the Twelve Apostles and the Seventy in 1835."

*Note: Regarding the first three ordinations, Heber C. Kimball recorded: "After we had thus been ordained by these brethren (Three Witnesses), the First Presidency laid their hands on us and confirmed these blessings and ordinations, and likewise predicted many things which should come to pass."[1]

---

1.   Heber C. Kimball, *Times and Seasons*, vi, 868.

Appendix E

Heavenly Visitations Received by the Prophet Joseph Smith

Personage	Selected References	Keys given or nature or appearance
God the Father	JS—H 1:17; HC 1:5; D&C 76:2, etc.	Opened this dispensation, introduced the Son
Jesus Christ	JS—H 1:17; HC 1:5–6; D&C 76:20–24; 110:2–10	Called Joseph as a prophet; accepted the temple
Moroni	JS—H 1:30–49, 59; JD 17:374	Tutored Joseph; gave keys of stick of Ephraim
John the Baptist	D&C 13:1; HC 1:39–42	Restored Aaronic Priesthood and its keys
Peter, James, John	D&C 27:12; 128:20; JD 18:326; HC 1:40–42	Restored Melchizedek Priesthood and apostleship and keys
Moses	D&C 110:11; JD 21:65; 23:48	Restored keys of gathering and leading the ten tribes

Elias	D&C 27:6; 110:12; JD 23:48	Committed the "gospel of Abraham"
Elijah	D&C 110:13–16	Conferred sealing power
Adam (Michael)	HC 2:380; 3:388; D&C 128:21; JD 18:326; 21:94; 23:48	Restored keys (perhaps of the presidency over the earth)
Noah (Gabriel)	D&C 128:21; JD 21:94; 23:48	Restored keys (perhaps of the power to preach the gospel)
Raphael	D&C 128:21	Restored keys (perhaps of the dispensation of Enoch's day)
Various angels	D&C 128:21	Restored keys (all declaring their individual dispensation)
Lehi	JD 16:265–66	Ministered to him
Nephi	JD 21:161; 16:266; 17:374	Tutored Joseph; gave him keys
Mormon	JD 17:374	Tutored Joseph; gave him keys
Unnamed angel	D&C 27; HC 1:106	Taught concerning use of wine in the sacrament
Unnamed angel	Life of Heber C. Kimball;[28] Temples of the Most High	Sent to accept dedication of the Kirtland Temple
Unnamed angel	Biography and Family Records of Lorenzo Snow	Visited Joseph three times; commanded him to practice plural marriage, as previously revealed by the Lord.

Appendix F

Poetic Portrayal of Doctrine and Covenants 76

[1]
I will go, I will go, to the home of the Saints,
Where the virtue's the value, and life the reward;
But before I return to my former estate,
I must fulfill the mission I had from the Lord.

[2]
Wherefore, hear O ye heavens, and give ear O ye earth,
And rejoice, ye inhabitants, truly again;
For the Lord he is God, and his life never ends,
And besides him there ne'er was a Savior of men.

[3]
His ways are a wonder, his wisdom is great;
The extent of his doings there's none can unveil;
His purposes fail not; from age unto age
He still is the same, and his years never fail.

[4]
His throne is the heavens—his life-time is all
Of eternity now, and eternity then;
His union is power, and none stays his hand,
The Alpha, Omega, for ever. Amen.

[5]

For thus saith the Lord, in the spirit of truth,
I am merciful, gracious, and good unto those
That fear me, and live for the life that's to come:
My delight is to honour the Saints with repose,

[6]

That serve me in righteousness true to the end;
Eternal's their glory and great their reward.
I'll surely reveal all my myst'ries to them—
The great hidden myst'ries in my kingdom stor'd;

[7]

From the council in Kolob, to time on the earth,
And for ages to come unto them I will show
My pleasure and will, what the kingdom will do:
Eternity's wonders they truly shall know.

[8]

Great things of the future I'll show unto them,
Yea, things of the vast generations to rise;
For their wisdom and glory shall be very great,
And their pure understanding extend to the skies.

[9]

And before them the wisdom of wise men shall cease,
And the nice understanding of prudent ones fail!
For the light of my spirit shall light mine elect,
And the truth is so mighty 'twill ever prevail.

[10]

And the secrets and plans of my will I'll reveal,
The sanctifi'd pleasures when earth is renew'd;
What the eye hath not seen, nor the ear hath yet heard,
Nor the heart of the natural man ever view'd.

[11]

I, Joseph, the prophet, in spirit beheld,
And the eyes of the inner man truly did see
Eternity sketch'd in a vision from God,
Of what was, and now is, and yet is to be.

[12]
Those things which the Father ordained of old,
Before the world was or a system had run;
Through Jesus, the Maker and Savior of all—
The only begotten (Messiah) his son.

[13]
Of whom I bear record, as all prophets have,
And the record I bear is the fulness—yea, even
The truth of the gospel of Jesus—the Christ,
With whom I convers'd in the vision of heav'n.

[14]
For while in the act of translating his word,
Which the Lord in his grace had appointed to me,
I came to the gospel recorded by John,
Chapter fifth, and the twenty-ninth verse which you'll see.

[15]
I marvell'd at these resurrections, indeed,
For it came unto me by the spirit direct:
And while I did meditate what it all meant,
The Lord touch'd the eyes of my own intellect.

[16]
Hosanna, for ever! They open'd anon,
And the glory of God shone around where I was;
And there was the Son at the Father's right hand,
In a fulness of glory and holy applause.

[17]
I beheld round the throne holy angels and hosts,
And sanctified beings from the worlds that have been,
In holiness worshipping God and the Lamb,
For ever and ever. Amen and amen.

[18]
And now after all of the proofs made of him,
By witnesses truly, by whom he was known,
This is mine, last of all, that he lives; yea, he lives!
And sits at the right hand of God on his throne.

[19]

And I heard a great voice bearing record from heav'n,
He's the Saviour and only begotten of God;
By him, of him, and through him, the worlds were all made,
Even all that career in the heavens so broad.

[20]

Whose inhabitants, too, from the first to the last,
Are sav'd by the very same Saviour of ours;
And, of course, are begotten God's daughters and sons
By the very same truths and the very same powers.

[21]

And I saw and bear record of warfare in heaven;
For an angel of light, in authority great,
Rebell'd against Jesus and sought for his power,
But was thrust down to woe from his glorified state.

[22]

And the heavens all wept, and the tears dropp'd like dew,
That Lucifer, son of the morning, had fell!
Yea, is fallen! is fallen and become, oh, alas!
The son of perdition, the devil of hell!

[23]

And while I was yet in the spirit of truth,
The commandment was—"Write ye the vision all out,
For Satan, old serpent, the devil's for war,
And yet will encompass the Saints round about."

[24]

And I saw, too, the suff'ring and misery of those
(Overcome by the devil, in warfare and fight)
In hell-fire and vengeance—the doom of the damn'd;
For the Lord said the vision is further, so write:

[25]

For thus saith the Lord, now concerning all those,
Who know of my power and partake of the same;
And suffer themselves that they be overcome
By the power of Satan, despising my name—

[26]
Defying my power, and denying the truth:
They are they of the world, or of men most forlorn,
The sons of perdition, of whom, ah! I say,
'Twere better for them had they never been born.

[27]
They're the vessels of wrath, and dishonour to God,
Doom'd to suffer his wrath in the regions of woe,
Through all the long night of eternity's round,
With the devil and all of his angels below.

[28]
Of whom it is said no forgiveness is found,
In this world, alas! nor the world that's to come,
For they have deny'd the spirit of God,
After having receiv'd it, and mis'ry's their doom.

[29]
And denying the only begotten of God,
And crucify him to themselves, as they do,
And openly put him to shame in their flesh,
By the gospel they cannot repentance renew.

[30]
They are they who go to the great lake of fire,
Which burneth with brimstone, yet never consumes,
And dwell with the devil, and angels of his,
While eternity goes and eternity comes.

[31]
They are they who must groan through the great second death,
And are not redeemed in the time of the Lord;
While all the rest are, through the triumph of Christ,
Made partakers of grace, by the power of his word.

[32]
The myst'ry of godliness truly is great;
The past, and the present, and what is to be;
And this is the gospel—glad tidings to all,
Which the voice from the heavens bore record to me:

[33]
That he came to the world in the middle of time,
To lay down his life for his friends and his foes,
And bear away sin as a mission of love,
And sanctify earth for a blessed repose.

[34]
'Tis decreed that he'll save all the work of his hands,
And sanctify them by his own precious blood;
And purify earth for the Sabbath of rest,
By the agent of fire as it was by the flood.

[35]
The Saviour will save all his Father did give,
Even all that he gave in the regions abroad,
Save the sons of perdition—they are lost, ever lost!
And can never return to the presence of God.

[36]
They are they who must reign with the devil in hell,
In eternity now, and eternity then!
Where the worm dieth not, and the fire is not quench'd,
And the punishment still is eternal. Amen.

[37]
And which is the torment apostates receive,
But the end or the place where the torment began,
Save to them who are made to partake of the same,
Was never, nor will be revealed unto man.

[38]
Yet God, by a vision, shows a glimpse of their fate,
And straightway he closes the scene that was shown;
So the width, or the depth, or the misery thereof,
Save to those that partake, is forever unknown.

[39]
And while I was pondering, the vision was closed,
And the voice said to me, write the vision; for, lo!
'Tis the end of the scene of the sufferings of those
Who remain filthy still in their anguish and woe.

[40]
And again I bear record of heavenly things,
Where virtue's the value above all that is priz'd,
Of the truth of the gospel concerning the just,
That rise in the first resurrection of Christ.

[41]
Who receiv'd, and believ'd, and repented likewise,
And then were baptiz'd, as a man always was,
Who ask'd and receiv'd a remission of sin,
And honoured the kingdom by keeping its laws.

[42]
Being buried in water, as Jesus had been,
And keeping the whole of his holy commands,
They received the gift of the spirit of truth,
By the ordinance truly of laying on hands.

[43]
For these overcome, by their faith and their works,
Being tried in their life-time, as purified gold,
And seal'd by the spirit of promise to life,
By men called of God, as was Aaron of old.

[44]
They are they, of the church of the first-born of God,
And unto whose hands he committeth all things;
For they hold the keys of the kingdom of heav'n,
And reign with the Saviour, as priests and as kings.

[45]
They're priests of the order of Melchizedek,
Like Jesus (from whom is this highest reward),
Receiving a fulness of glory and light;
As written—they're Gods even sons of the Lord.

[46]
So all things are theirs; yea, of life or of death;
Yea, whether things now, or to come, all are theirs,
And they are the Saviour's, and he is the Lord's,
Having overcome all, as eternity's heirs.

[47]

'Tis wisdom that man never glory in man,
But give God the glory for all that he hath;
For the righteous will walk in the presence of God,
While the wicked are trod underfoot in his wrath.

[48]

Yea, the righteous shall dwell in the presence of God,
And of Jesus, forever, from earth's second birth—
For when he comes down in the splendour of heav'n,
All those he'll bring with him to reign on the earth.

[49]

These are they that arise in their bodies of flesh,
When the trump of the first resurrection shall sound;
These are they that come up to Mount Zion, in life,
Where the blessings and gifts of the spirit abound.

[50]

These are they that have come to the heavenly place;
To the numberless courses of angels above:
To the city of God, e'en the holiest of all,
And the home of the blessed, the fountain of love;

[51]

To the church of old Enoch, and of the first-born:
And gen'ral assembly of ancient renown'd,
Whose names are all kept in the archives of heav'n,
As chosen and faithful, and fit to be crown'd.

[52]

These are they that are perfect through Jesus' own blood,
whose bodies celestial are mention'd by Paul,
where the sun is the typical glory thereof,
And God, and his Christ, are the true judge of all.

[53]

Again, I beheld the terrestrial world,
In the order and glory of Jesus go on;
'Twas not as the church of the first-born of God,
But shone in its place, as the moon to the sun,

[54]
Behold, these are they that have died without law;
The heathen of ages that never had hope,
And those of the region and shadow of death,
The spirits in prison, that light has brought up.

[55]
To spirits in prison the Saviour once preach'd,
And taught them the gospel, with powers afresh;
And then were the living baptiz'd for their dead,
That they might be judg'd as if men in the flesh.

[56]
These are they that are hon'rable men of the earth;
Who were blinded and dup'd by the cunning of men;
They receiv'd not the truth of the Saviour at first;
But did, when they heard it in prison again.

[57]
Not valiant for truth, they obtain'd not the crown,
But are of that glory that's typ'd by the moon:
They are they, that come into the presence of Christ,
But not to the fulness of God on his throne.

[58]
Again, I beheld the telestial, as third,
The lesser, or starry world, next in its place,
For the leaven must leaven three measures of meal,
And every knee bow that is subject to grace.

[59]
These are they that receiv'd not the gospel of Christ,
Or evidence, either, that he ever was;
As the stars are all diff'rent in glory and light,
So differs the glory of these by the laws.

[60]
These are they that deny not the spirit of God,
But are thrust down to hell, with the devil, for sins,
As hypocrites, liars, whoremongers and thieves,
And stay 'till the last resurrection begins.

[61]
'Till the Lamb shall have finish'd the work he begun;
Shall have trodden the winepress in fury alone.
And overcome all by the pow'r of his might:
He conquers to conquer, and saves all his own.

[62]
These are they that receive not a fulness of light,
From Christ, in eternity's world, where they are,
The terrestial sends them the Comforter, though,
And minist'ring angels, to happify there.

[63]
And so the telestial is minister'd to,
By ministers from the terrestrial one,
As terrestrial is, from the celestial throne;
And the great, greater, greatest, seem's stars, moon, and sun.

[64]
And thus I beheld, in the vision of heav'n,
The telestial glory, dominion and bliss,
Surpassing the great understanding of men,—
Unknown, save reveal'd, in a world vain as this.

[65]
And lo! I beheld the terrestrial, too,
Which excels the telestial in glory and light,
In splendour and knowledge, and wisdom and joy,
In blessings and graces, dominion and might.

[66]
I beheld the celestial, in glory sublime;
Which is the most excellent kingdom that is,
Where God, e'en the Father, in harmony reigns;
Almighty, supreme, and eternal in bliss.

[67]
Where the church of the first-born in union reside,
And they see as they're seen, and they know as they're known
Being equal in power, dominion and might,
With a fulness of glory and grace round his throne.

[68]
The glory celestial is one like the sun;
The glory terrestrial is one like the moon;
The glory telestial is one like the stars,
And all harmonize like the parts of a tune.

[69]
As the stars are all different in lustre and size,
So the telestial region is mingled in bliss;
From the least unto greatest, and greatest to least,
The reward is exactly as promised in this.

[70]
These are they that came out for Apollos and Paul;
For Cephas and Jesus, in all kinds of hope;
For Enoch and Moses, and Peter and John;
For Luther and Calvin, and even the Pope.

[71]
For they never received the gospel of Christ
Nor the prophetic spirit that came from the Lord;
Nor the covenant neither, which Jacob once had;
They went their own way, and they have their reward.

[72]
By the order of God, last of all, these are they,
That will not be gather'd with saints here below,
To be caught up to Jesus, and meet in the cloud:
In darkness they worshipp'd; to darkness they go.

[73]
These are they that are sinful, the wicked at large,
That glutted their passion by meanness or worth;
All liars, adulterers, sorcerers, and proud,
And suffer as promis'd, God's wrath on the earth.

[74]
These are they that must suffer the vengeance of hell,
'Till Christ shall have trodden all enemies down,
And perfected his work, in the fulness of time,
And is crowned on his throne with his glorious crown.

[75]
The vast multitude of the telestial world—
As the stars of the skies, or the sands of the sea;
The voice of Jehovah echo'd far and wide,
Every tongue shall confess and they all bow the knee.

[76]
Ev'ry man shall be judg'd by the works of his life,
And receive a reward in the mansions prepar'd;
For his judgments are just, and his works never end,
As his prophets and servants have always declar'd.

[77]
But the great things of God, which he show'd unto rile,
Unlawful to utter, I dare not declare;
They surpass all the wisdom and greatness of men,
And only are seen, as has Paul where they are.

[78]
I will go, I will go, while the secret of life,
Is blooming in heaven, and blasting in hell;
Is leaving on earth, and a-budding in space:
I will go, I will go, with you, brother, farewell.

Appendix G

John Whitmer's History after the November Conferences

Following the revelations recorded in sections 69 and 70, John traveled to Missouri with Oliver where he remained and continued as Church historian. He was one of the leading brethren who offered himself to the mob in Jackson County to help end the violence and was later expelled from the county along with the rest of the Saints in November 1833, joining those who had fled to Clay County, and other surrounding counties. In 1834 he was appointed a member of the Missouri Church Presidency, a stake presidency of sorts, with his brother, David, and William W. Phelps. He was editor of the *LDS Messenger and Advocate* in Kirtland in 1835–1836 and participated in the Kirtland Temple dedication. He helped establish the Latter-day Saints in Far West, Missouri, in 1836–1837 but in March 1838 was excommunicated, along with several other prominent Church leaders, based on an accusation of financial wrongdoing related to the sale of Church properties. In recording this event in the record history "The History of John Whitmer," he wrote, "Some temperal movements, have not proved satisfactory to all parties has also terminated in the expulsion of [many] members, among whom is W. W. Phelps and myself. Therefore I close the history of the church of Latter Day Saints, hoping that . . . I find favor in the eyes of God."

Two months later, he received a letter from Joseph and Sidney asking him to relinquish his history, a request he refused. John Corrill and Elias Higbee were called to take his place. Within three weeks of John's refusal to relinquish his history, Joseph began recording his own history, assisted by two others—Sidney Rigdon and his scribe, George W. Robinson.

John was forced to leave Far West and move to Richmond County, Missouri, in June 1838 but returned after the Saints were expelled from Missouri. At some point, John crossed out the closing words from his history, removed his name from the list of excommunicated Saints he had written, and then, continued his record by writing unfounded accusations coming out of Nauvoo.

Despite any affiliation with the Church in Nauvoo and in the West, he remained connected to the Restoration. After the martyrdom of Joseph Smith, he wrote support for the claims of James J. Strang in his history, but later crossed them out. In September 1847, acting on William E. McLellin's initiatives, John met with his brother, David, and William at Far West, attempting to reconstitute the Church of Christ with David as president. In fact, John, David, and their brother-in-law, Hiram Page, received ordination in this newly founded organization. However, a full implementation did not occur until the 1870s, and its adherents amounted only to a small group that associated with the Whitmers in Missouri and a few others in Kirtland.

John maintained his testimony as a witness of the Book of Mormon in letters, newspapers articles, and Sunday services until the end of his life in 1878. Despite the many contributions he made to the Restoration, John is practically ignored in many historical treatments, or when he is not, he is often given a "bad rap." This unfortunate characterization has left many Latter-day Saints unaware of the critical role he played in early Church history.

About the Authors

DAMON BAHR

Damon L. Bahr is an associate professor at Brigham Young University. He took a year's leave of absence from BYU to serve a mission in Kirtland, Ohio, with his wife, Kim.

Having spent several years studying the Kirtland, Ohio, period in Church history, including the Johnson Home year, it was their privilege to spend most of their mission helping provide tours for over 1,300 people of the historic Johnson Home, and it was during that time that his love for the Johnson Home and what happened there deepened and provided an impetus for this book.

Damon earned bachelors' and doctorate degrees at BYU and a master's from Utah State University.

THOMAS P. AARDEMA

Thomas P. Aardema is a region director of seminaries and institutes. He serves as the bishop of the Hiram Ohio Ward. He has a BA, MBA, and PhD. He and his wife, Emilee, are the parents of five boys.